SHARKS
AND OTHER SCARY
SEA CREATURES

By
Dr Miranda MacQuitty

Consultant
Dr Philip Whitfield

A Dorling Kindersley Book

Dorling **DK** Kindersley

LONDON, NEW YORK, SYDNEY, DELHI,
PARIS, MUNICH, and JOHANNESBURG

Editor Lucy Hurst
Designer Polly Appleton
Senior Editor Fran Jones
Senior Art Editor Stefan Podhorodecki
Category Publisher Jayne Parsons
Managing Art Editor Jacquie Gulliver
Picture Researcher Jo Haddon
DK Pictures Rose Horridge and Sarah Mills
Production Erica Rosen
DTP Designer Siu Yin Ho
Jacket Designer Dean Price

First published in Great Britain in 2002 by
Dorling Kindersley Limited
80 Strand, London WC2R 0RL

A Penguin Company

2 4 6 8 10 9 7 5 3 1

The CIP Catalogue record for this book
is available from the British Library

ISBN 0-7513-3753-6

Reproduced by Colourscan, Singapore
Printed and bound by L.E.G.O., Italy

See our complete catalogue at

www.dk.com

CONTENTS

INTRODUCTION

A fin slicing through water, jaws armed with razor-sharp teeth, and a mean-looking grin – no wonder we think sharks are frightening! But, there's more to sharks than this scary image. Travel into the world of these skillful hunters to discover how they use their powerful bodies and senses to hunt prey. Also take the opportunity to meet other sea creatures with the skill to kill.

Do sharks deserve their reputation as bloodthirsty killers? People who study sharks certainly don't think so. There are at least 400 species of shark and most of them are harmless. In the pages that follow you'll find out how sharks have earned their deadly reputation, but how it's actually people who pose the biggest threat to shark survival. Learn how sharks have a rubbery skeleton and rough outer skin that makes them different from other fish.

THE GREAT WHITE SHARK'S STREAMLINED BODY AND SHARP TEETH MAKE IT A FEROCIOUS HUNTER.

Discover, too, that sharks range in size from a massive 12 m (39 ft) to one that would fit into the palm of an adult's hand.

These creatures have superb senses to track down prey, with an extraordinary ability to detect the smell of blood and the sound of splashing from a distance. Find out about shark teeth and how they are perfectly designed for grasping and biting their favourite foods. How sharks mate is revealed, along with which ones give birth to pups.

RAYS ARE CLOSELY RELATED TO SHARKS, BUT HAVE MANY DIFFERENCES TOO.

See an amazing array of shark relatives from stingrays to sawfish. Learn about other scary sea creatures from venomous fish and stinging jellies to the weird-looking monsters of the deep.

All sea creatures – scary or not – are under threat. The balance of sea life is altered by overfishing, while chemicals and oil spills poison marine animals and plants. See what you can do to help at the end of the book. The more we learn about the sea, the more we will respect and cherish it.

If you would like to find out more, why not explore some of the exciting websites that appear throughout the book in the black Log On "bites". These top websites provide great information about the fascinating world of sharks and the sea.

Miranda MacQuitty

MEET THE SHARKS

Most people would rather not come face to face with a shark, which isn't surprising. They are sophisticated hunters with remarkable senses and bigger brains than most other fish. They also sport a scary set of teeth! A shark's streamlined shape and powerful body helps it to speed through the water like a torpedo. You can think of sharks as the lions or tigers of the sea – the top predators – with few enemies apart from people.

A different kind of fish

One of the first things you need to know about sharks is how they differ from other fish. For example, sharks have no bones. Instead they have skeletons made of strong, flexible cartilage – just like the bendy bits inside your ears and nose. Most fish, such as tuna, have bone skeletons.

A BLUE SHARK HUNTS FOR PREY IN THE OCEAN OFF THE CALIFORNIAN COAST, USA.

But not every part of a shark's skeleton is rubbery. The backbone is reinforced with strengthening minerals, and is a strong framework for muscles to work against. Teeth are strong too, as they are made of dentine like ours.

On the outside, sharks are covered with tough and protective tooth-like scales called denticles, instead of the flat scales that you see on bony fish. Denticles can be shed and grown again – just like a shark's teeth. If you were unlucky enough to brush up against a shark, you'd notice that its skin feels rough like sandpaper.

CLOSE-UP OF SHARK SKIN DOTTED WITH THE DENTICLES THAT MAKE IT FEEL ROUGH.

Shark gills

Sharks also have a different system of breathing. Like all fish, a shark breathes by taking water in through its mouth and passing it over its gills. These do the same job as your lungs, extracting oxygen and passing it into the bloodstream.

But instead of having flaps over their gills, sharks have gill slits. Water streams out through these slits, which you can see between the shark's head and its front fins.

There are exceptions to this. Sharks that lie flat on the bottom of the ocean, such as angel sharks, can take in water through a hole behind their eye, called a spiracle, and then pass it out through their gills. This prevents their gills from clogging up with sand – ouch!

Shark fins

As they cruise along, sharks hold their fins out from the

THIS HUGE WHALE SHARK GLIDES ALONG THE AUSTRALIAN COAST. IT IS KEPT IN MID-WATER, DESPITE ITS BIG SIZE, BECAUSE OF ITS BODY SHAPE AND OILY LIVER.

GILL SLITS

sides of their bodies. Water passing over the front fins – called pectorals – lifts the shark up at the front. This has the same effect as air passing over an aeroplane wing. To propel a shark forward, its tail fin beats from side to side. At the same time, the fins on the shark's back stabilize it, preventing it from rolling over in the water.

Sink or swim

That all works fine while a shark is moving, but if it stopped swimming it would gradually sink. This is because sharks are heavier than water. Sharks can't adjust their buoyancy like bony fish that have a gas-filled swim bladder – like a balloon – inside them. Instead, sharks have a large oily liver that helps them stay in mid-water. Because oil is lighter than water, the liver lifts the shark up towards the surface.

Sharks that spend a lot of time at the surface, such as whale sharks and basking sharks, have massive livers that are like big floats. This means they can swim slowly without sinking.

Great and small

These shark features relate to most sharks, but within the shark world there is a great variety of species – more than 400 in fact. Of these, there is no contest over which is the largest shark in the ocean – its the whale shark, which also happens to be the world's largest fish. It grows more than 12 m (39 ft) long and is bigger than a double-decker bus. Luckily for us, these giants are interested in eating plankton, not people! The second largest shark, the basking shark,

Fast sharks

Neither the biggest nor smallest are the fastest sharks. This honour goes to the great white, porbeagle, and mako, which have crescent-shaped tail fins. The narrow shape of the tail fin reduces drag that could slow the shark down. A keel

THE FASTEST SHARKS ARE STREAMLINED LIKE TORPEDOES

grows to about 10 m (33 ft), which is still enormous.

At the other end of the scale, the record for the world's smallest shark is currently held by the dwarf lantern shark, which can fit in the palm of a man's hand. The spined pygmy shark and the pygmy ribbontail catshark come close seconds.

DORSAL FIN STOPS THE SHARK FROM ROLLING ONTO ITS SIDE.

KEEL MAKES SHARK STREAMLINED

CRESCENT-SHAPED TAIL FIN

PELVIC FIN

PECTORAL FIN

running along the narrow base of the tail helps to make these sharks even more streamlined.

Another feature of fast sharks is that they keep their body temperature higher than the surrounding water. Staying warm probably helps their muscles to work better. This increases the shark's swimming speed, so it can catch speedy prey such as squid and seals.

The fastest is the shortfin mako that reaches speeds of up to 86 kmh (55 mph). Not much compared to a sports car you may think, but water is 800 times denser than air, so it is much harder to move through.

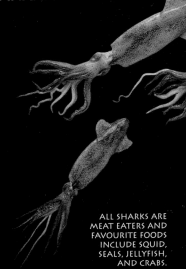

ALL SHARKS ARE MEAT EATERS AND FAVOURITE FOODS INCLUDE SQUID, SEALS, JELLYFISH, AND CRABS.

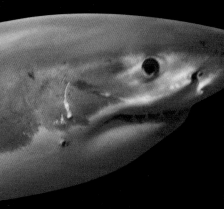

THE GREAT WHITE SHARK IS ONE OF THE FASTEST IN THE OCEAN. IT USES A BURST OF SPEED TO CHASE AND CATCH PREY.

Jumping sharks

Some sharks move so fast, they can leap right out of the water! They may use this skill to try and escape from a fishing line, or when chasing prey. The mako can leap 6 m (18 ft) out of the water. But, most amazing is the leap of the hefty great white shark as it hunts seal pups off Seal Island, South Africa. It gathers speed by charging up through the water, surprising the pups from below. The force carries the shark – and the unfortunate seal – right out of the water!

However fast or slow, big or small, each shark is perfectly designed to successfully hunt and devour its prey.

WHERE SHARKS LIVE

You could swim in any of the world's oceans, from the sunny surface and shallows to the dark depths, and be in shark territory. A few types of sharks even make their homes in lakes and rivers. To blend in with their surroundings, many sharks rely on camouflage to give them an element of surprise when hunting their prey.

Hot or cold water?

Different types of sharks are adapted to different water temperatures and generally need to stay within the right area to survive. Some like to for deeper, colder waters.

The great white, starry smoothhound, and horn sharks like living in water that's not too hot or too cold. For example, the starry smoothhound lives

WHITETIP REEF SHARKS CAN STACK ON TOP OF EACH OTHER TO REST

swim where it's warm, such as the whale sharks that live in the tropical waters of the Atlantic, Pacific, and Indian oceans.

But other sharks, such as the Greenland shark, prefer cold water. In winter they live in the icy waters of the Arctic Ocean and neighbouring areas. In summer when the water gets warmer, they head

THREE WHITETIP REEF SHARKS REST IN A CAVE OFF THE COAST OF BURMA (MYANMAR) DURING THE DAY.

in the temperate waters off the coast of Northern Europe.

Near the shore

Sharks have never been the easiest of animals to watch or study, and those we get to know best are the ones that come close to land. Female lemon sharks, for example, come into sheltered water near the coast in the Bahamas to give birth. This is one of the rare occasions when people have seen shark pups being born.

Tiger sharks also come close to land in order to feed on young albatrosses in Pacific Island lagoons. Any young birds that misjudge their first flight are snapped up if they falter and tumble into the water.

Reef sharks

Snorkellers and scuba divers may see some of the beautiful reef sharks that hunt around corals. The blacktip reef shark lives in the shallow water over reefs and in coral lagoons, while the grey reef shark lives in deeper water, such as along channels and outer reefs. The whitetip reef shark rests under ledges and in caves during the day. It generally hunts at night, poking its snout around corals in search of fish, octopuses, crabs, and lobsters.

LOG ON...
www.enchantedlearning.com/subjects/sharks/

Sea floor dwellers

Many types of sharks live on or near the bottom of shallow coastal waters. Horn sharks rest together in rocky crevices during the day, and then at night they look for food such as shellfish on the sea floor.

Nurse sharks could be seen as the lazy sharks because they spend much of the day resting on the sandy sea floor, often near coral reefs. When they get peckish, they are like giant vacuum cleaners, sucking prey off the sea floor or from between rocks. Bamboo sharks have extra-flexible bodies so they can curl right up to rest in coral crevices and tide pools.

Camouflaged sharks

Other sea floor sharks are exceptionally flat – so much so that you'd think they were part of the sea floor! Being flat helps some sharks stay camouflaged. For example, wobbegong and angel sharks are just the right shape to lie there, ready to ambush any unwary fish or crab passing by. Wobbegongs have

WEIRD WORLD

AUSTRALIAN ABORIGINALS GAVE WOBBEGONG SHARKS THEIR UNUSUAL NAME. THEY'RE COMMONLY FOUND IN SHALLOW AREAS IN THE WESTERN PACIFIC.

THE WOBBEGONG LIVES ON THE OCEAN FLOOR – JUST LIKE A SEA CARPET. CAN YOU MAKE OUT ITS EYES ON TOP OF ITS HEAD?

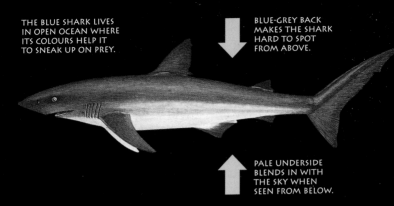

THE BLUE SHARK LIVES
IN OPEN OCEAN WHERE
ITS COLOURS HELP IT
TO SNEAK UP ON PREY.

BLUE-GREY BACK
MAKES THE SHARK
HARD TO SPOT
FROM ABOVE.

PALE UNDERSIDE
BLENDS IN WITH
THE SKY WHEN
SEEN FROM BELOW.

colourful markings and leafy bits of skin around their heads which allow them to blend in with weed-covered rocks or coral reefs. Angel sharks go one step further by becoming part of the sea floor. They shuffle down into the sand and become harder to see.

Open ocean

Sharks that live further out to sea also use camouflage. The sharks living in the surface waters, such as the blue shark, pelagic thresher, and mako, have bluish grey backs and light-coloured bellies. Their backs blend in with the sea when viewed from above, and their bellies blend in with the sky when viewed from below. This colouring

gives them a chance to sneak up on their prey without being seen.

Deep-water sharks

If you took a submersible down to the depths, you probably wouldn't see a shark unless you put out bait. Few sharks can live in deep water as there just isn't enough food for them to eat. Occasionally, though, sharks have been spotted at depths

To the surface and back

Some sharks live in deep water during the day, and then travel up to feed in shallower mid-water at night. The spined pygmy does this to follow its dinner – squid and fish – which makes the same journey. These sharks then feed near the surface, using the cover of darkness

MANY DEEP-SEA SHARKS ARE HIDDEN BY THEIR DARK COLOURS

of more than 4 km (2.5 miles).

Sharks that do live in deep water don't always look like typical sharks. For example, the birdbeak dogfish has a long snout and huge eyes that help it to see in the gloomy water.

Another deep-water shark, the goblin shark, looks equally strange. Its long snout, beady eyes, and pinkish-grey skin look spooky! It swims about hunting other creatures deep in the Atlantic, Pacific, and Indian oceans.

A DEEP-SEA CAT SHARK PHOTOGRAPHED IN THE DEEP WATER OFF THE GALAPAGOS ISLANDS.

to surprise their prey.

Another shark with similar habits is the megamouth, which lives more than 200 m (660 ft) below the ocean's surface. At night, it travels slowly upwards to feed on shrimp-like krill, jellyfish, and other tasty morsels drifting near the surface waters. The megamouth is one of the rarest sharks, and was only discovered in the 1970s. It's unusual that such a large shark – more than 5 m (16 ft) long – was not discovered for such a long time.

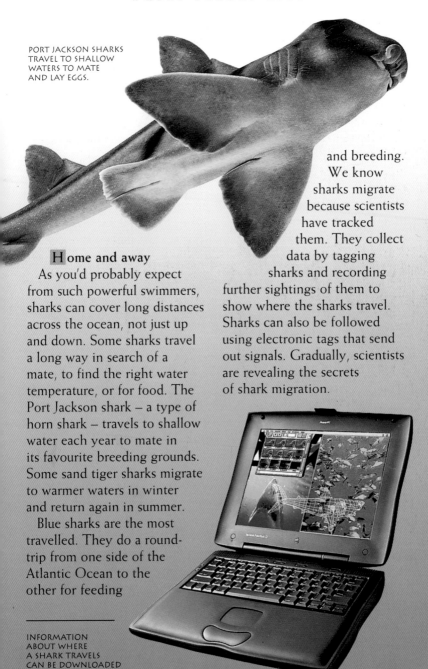

PORT JACKSON SHARKS TRAVEL TO SHALLOW WATERS TO MATE AND LAY EGGS.

Home and away

As you'd probably expect from such powerful swimmers, sharks can cover long distances across the ocean, not just up and down. Some sharks travel a long way in search of a mate, to find the right water temperature, or for food. The Port Jackson shark – a type of horn shark – travels to shallow water each year to mate in its favourite breeding grounds. Some sand tiger sharks migrate to warmer waters in winter and return again in summer.

Blue sharks are the most travelled. They do a round-trip from one side of the Atlantic Ocean to the other for feeding

and breeding. We know sharks migrate because scientists have tracked them. They collect data by tagging sharks and recording further sightings of them to show where the sharks travel. Sharks can also be followed using electronic tags that send out signals. Gradually, scientists are revealing the secrets of shark migration.

INFORMATION ABOUT WHERE A SHARK TRAVELS CAN BE DOWNLOADED ONTO A COMPUTER.

19

Freshwater sharks

Sharks seem to live almost everywhere in the ocean, and some species can even live in rivers and lakes. The bull shark has been found 3,000 km (1,860 miles) up the Amazon. It has also been spotted in the Mississippi in the USA, and the Zambezi in Africa. Bull sharks swim upriver from the sea, and are able to move from sea to freshwater by regulating salt and other substances in their blood. Some sharks swim so far up rivers that they reach lakes, such as Lake Nicaragua in Central America.

Finding river sharks is a challenge. Some, such as the speartooth shark, are becoming rare because their river habitats are threatened by development.

Travelling companions

Wherever a shark goes, a little band of travelling companions joins in. It is hard to imagine seeking out the company of sharks, but pilotfish and young golden trevally fish like to tag along. By swimming next to big sharks, these small fish are safe from other big fish that might eat them. Sounds risky, but they're swift enough to keep clear of a shark's jaws.

Shark suckers

Remoras are another type of companion who literally hitch a ride! They have ridged suckers on their heads that they use to clamp on to large sharks. Remoras are lazy because they can swim perfectly well by themselves. Apart from free transport, remoras also get to snack on any bits of food that don't make it into the shark's mouth.

Small types of remoras act as cleaners by nibbling skin parasites off sharks. Brave ones even go inside a whale shark's mouth and gills where they probably nibble off the parasites that irritate the shark.

Whether harmful or helpful to the shark, its fellow travellers are well suited to their particular way of making a living.

WEIRD WORLD
NOT ALL CREATURES THAT TRAVEL WITH SHARKS ARE FRIENDLY. PARASITES, SUCH AS THESE SHRIMP-LIKE COPEPODS, SCRAPE AWAY AT A SHARK'S SKIN AND EAT IT, IRRITATING THE SHARK.

REMORAS ATTACH THEMSELVES TO THE UNDERSIDE OF A WHALE SHARK.

21

SUPERB SENSES

One of the main reasons sharks are so successful is their sophisticated senses. Sharks smell, taste, touch, see, and hear, but can also pick up electrical signals generated by their prey. A shark's senses are well-tuned, whether it's a speedy hunter, a lie-in-wait predator, or a sluggish seeker of food along the sea floor. Sharks also use senses to identify threats, meet a mate, and find their way.

Sense of smell

Smell is an important shark sense. Like us, sharks smell with their nostrils, but they don't breathe through them. Instead, sea water streams through a shark's nostrils as it swims along, bringing chemical clues about what's in the water. At the back of the nostrils there are bag-like structures that contain leafy folds. As the sea water flows up the

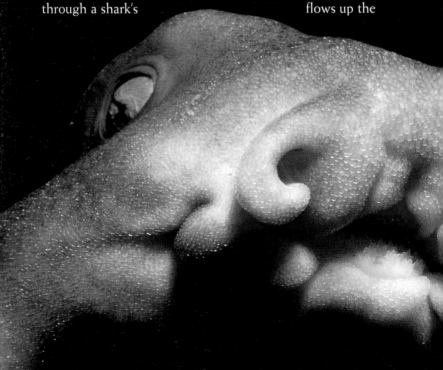

nostrils and between the folds, chemicals in the water bind to the surface of the folds. These chemicals trigger nerve signals that zip off to the shark's brain for processing, telling the shark which of its favourite foods is swimming nearby.

Smells in water
A shark's sense of smell is so good it can detect tiny concentrations of blood that have been diluted more than a million times. Sharks can smell

A SHARK USES ITS SHARP SENSE OF SMELL TO DETECT BLEEDING OR INJURED ANIMALS THAT MAKE EASY PREY.

SMELL IS ONE OF THE MAIN SENSES SHARKS USE TO FIND FOOD

and identify many other things too – for example tests have shown that the blacktip reef shark can smell one drop of fish extract in the equivalent of an Olympic-sized swimming pool. But it depends when it last ate.

HORN SHARKS, LIKE THIS PORT JACKSON SHARK, HAVE WELL-DEVELOPED NOSTRILS AND A KEEN SENSE OF SMELL.

Amazingly, the hungrier a shark, the better it is at detecting the smell of fish. A shark may smell an injured animal hundreds of metres away. Once the smell registers in the shark's brain it thinks "goody, grub's up", and swims

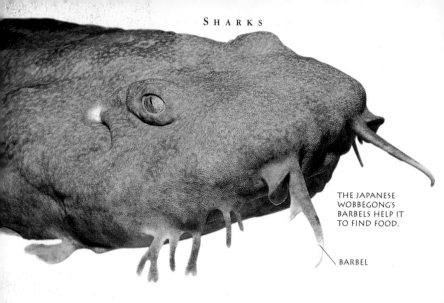

THE JAPANESE
WOBBEGONG'S
BARBELS HELP IT
TO FIND FOOD.

BARBEL

back and forth following the direction of the odour, until it homes in on the injured animal.

Taste buds

Smell works at a distance, but for a shark to really know if it likes something, it has to take a bite or attempt to swallow it. Once there's food inside its mouth, a shark uses the taste buds in its mouth and gullet, and on its tongue – although not all sharks have tongues. Sharks are not known for their table manners, and if a shark doesn't like the taste of what it's eaten – it spits it out.

Touchy feely

Some sharks may be able to taste and feel using a pair of feelers, called barbels, on the end of their snout. Nurse

sharks, bamboo sharks, and wobbegongs are among those that have barbels. These are very useful for feeling around for buried prey, and possibly tasting it too if they have taste receptors on their barbels.

Sharks also have nerve endings under their skin that are sensitive to touch. So it's never a good idea to poke a shark! These nerve endings

WEIRD WORLD
SOME FISH ARE SPECIALLY ADAPTED SO THAT A SHARK WON'T LIKE THE TASTE OF THEM AND WILL LEAVE THEM ALONE. THE FINLESS SOLE, FOR EXAMPLE, CLEVERLY COATS ITSELF WITH SLIME THAT TASTES HORRIBLE TO SHARKS.

keep the shark aware of its own body by letting it know how much its fins and body are moving.

E ye spy

As well as great senses of smell, taste, and touch, sharks also have exceptional eyesight. A shark's eyes are usually located on each side of its head, although some sea-floor dwelling sharks have eyes on the top of their heads. Hammerhead sharks have eyes on the far edges of their T-shaped heads, which they swing from side to side for a better view.

LOG ON...

www.discovery.com / area/nature/sharks/sharks1.htm

CLOSE-UP OF A NURSE SHARK'S EYE. THE IRIS (WHITE) CONTRACTS OR EXPANDS TO ALLOW IN DIFFERENT LEVELS OF LIGHT.

SOME SHRIMPS MAKE SNAPPING NOISES THAT MAY ATTRACT THE ATTENTION OF SHARKS.

Night vision

Sharks have excellent eyesight in the dark, and see ten times better than we can in dim light. This means they can hunt during the half-light of dawn and dusk, or at night. Sharks can see well in the dark because a mirror-like layer at the back of each eye bounces light rays back, making the most of the available light. This reflection of light also means that if you shine a light on a shark's eyes in the dark, they would light up yellow or green like the eyes of a cat.

Daytime sight

Sharks also see well during the day, and have pupils that adapt to different amounts of light, just like ours. When the iris opens up, the pupil gets larger and lets in more light, but if the iris closes, the pupil gets smaller and lets in less light. This is unusual in fish.

Although they are underwater, sharks can see the intensity of different shades, and some are known to see in colour. Deep-water sharks have adapted to see well in blue light, because blue is the part of the light spectrum that penetrates the deepest in the ocean.

Shut eye

Another thing about shark sight is that some, including the blue and lemon sharks, have a third eyelid that draws across the eye. They close this third eyelid when hunting or if poked in the eye but their "normal" eyelids don't close. The great white shark doesn't have a third eyelid but it does roll its eyes back in their sockets when attacking prey. This protects the more delicate front part of the eye from damage if the prey pokes the shark in the eye while struggling to escape.

Noisy sea

Seeing may be different underwater but so is hearing. This is because sounds travel better in water than on land. The sea is full of weird noises, such as shrimps snapping or whales singing. Sharks don't make many noises themselves, apart from crunching up their prey with their big teeth. But sharks use their sense of hearing all the time to help them find their prey. They can hear sounds from more than 250 m (700 ft) away, and are especially sensitive to the sound of splashing made by an injured fish or mammal.

Ear inside

In order to hear these sounds, sharks have ears. However, you might not recognize them as they don't have the outer ear flaps of cartilage that our ears have. But inside their heads, a shark's inner ear is a bit like ours, except that it is connected to a tiny fluid-filled canal. This canal opens to the outside on either side of the shark's head. Sound waves travel through the water and down the canal to the inner ear. Here, sensors send messages to the shark's brain, which interprets the noises as sounds.

The inner ear also lets the shark know the position of its body in the water in the same way that our ears help us to balance.

Good vibrations

Like other fish, sharks can detect vibrations in the water. They do

SOUNDS MADE UNDERWATER MOVE IN WAVES TOWARDS THIS STARRY SMOOTHHOUND SHARK'S EARS.

this using a line of sensory cells called a lateral line. This runs along the side of the body, and branches out around the head. Each sense cell sits in an opening that contains tiny hairs. These hairs detect any vibrations in the water. A shark can therefore sense water movement caused by another creature nearby – which might turn out to be prey or a predator. It also helps them avoid bumping into obstacles.

E lectric aura
The most amazing sense of all is the shark's ability to detect weak electricial signals made by other creatures. Muscle contractions, nerve signals, and the difference between body fluids and the surrounding sea water generate minuscule amounts of electricity. So every creature has a kind of electric aura – we just can't see it. Sharks sense this electricity through little jelly-filled holes, or pores, on their snouts. One of the best sharks at detecting

weak electricity is the hammerhead. It has an area dotted with lots of pores under its head.

U sing their spark
Sharks use this electrosense, as it is known, to find prey that lives in murky water or is hidden in the sand. Lie-in-wait predators may use their electrosense at night to work out when an animal gets within reach of their swift jaws. Sharks

HAMMERHEAD SHARKS HAVE A HIGHLY TUNED ELECTROSENSE

SCALLOPED HAMMERHEAD SHARKS MAY USE THEIR ELECTROSENSE TO DETECT LANDMARKS ON THE SEA FLOOR.

are not alone – a variety of other fish also have the ability to sense electric auras. They may also use it to communicate with others. For example, rays use electrosense to find a mate.

Finding their way

Electrosense may also help sharks to find their way. By sensing the difference between their own electric aura and the Earth's magnetic field, scientists think sharks take a compass reading to keep them travelling in one direction. The electrosense pores under the head of the scalloped hammerhead are widely placed, so they may even be able to detect different magnetic patterns on the sea floor. These could act as landmarks or even routes to a particular area.

A shark's extra sense, its electrosense, is important for its survival, but all senses are vital in the shark's hunt for prey.

JAWS!

The first thing you notice about sharks is their teeth – lots of 'em! Imagine seeing row after row of spiky teeth, packed into a huge, powerful jaw, opening up before you as you swim in the sea. Not all sharks are scary – some are shy or gentle – but they're all meat eaters at the top of the food chain. Sharks eat in different ways, devouring a variety of food from plankton to seals and other sharks – and sometimes even people!

Tooth replacement

Sharks are perhaps best known – and feared – for their amazing teeth. Whatever shape or size they are, a shark's teeth make it an efficient killer. What is worse (for their prey) is that a shark has a never-ending supply. New teeth move forward continuously, as though they are on a conveyor belt. Sharks can lose teeth when biting prey because their teeth are set into their gums but not secured into their jaws, like ours. Every time one is lost, a new one is ready to replace it. A shark can get through more than 30,000 teeth in its lifetime. And, because new teeth are always larger than the ones they replace, sharks look scarier as they grow older.

Most sharks replace just a few teeth at a time. Scientists observing young lemon sharks in captivity have noticed that it can take about eight days for all of their front teeth to be replaced. Other sharks, such as the Greenland shark, shed a whole row of teeth at once,

A CROSS-SECTION OF A MAKO SHARK'S JAW SHOWS THE CONVEYOR BELT OF SPIKY NEW TEETH GRADUALLY MOVING FORWARD.

so get a whole new set of pearly white gnashers every time.

Types of teeth

Each species of shark is equipped with the right shape of teeth for its favourite food. The curved spiky teeth of the sand tiger and mako shark are just the job to grip slippery fish or squid. A fully grown great white shark has triangular jagged-edged teeth that can carve big chunks of flesh from large animals, such as seals. Some sharks have blunt teeth that allow them to crunch through

WEIRD WORLD

TIGER SHARKS SWALLOW ALL KINDS OF "FOOD" – ONE EVEN HAD A CHICKEN COOP WITH THE REMAINS OF BONES AND FEATHERS INSIDE ITS STOMACH.

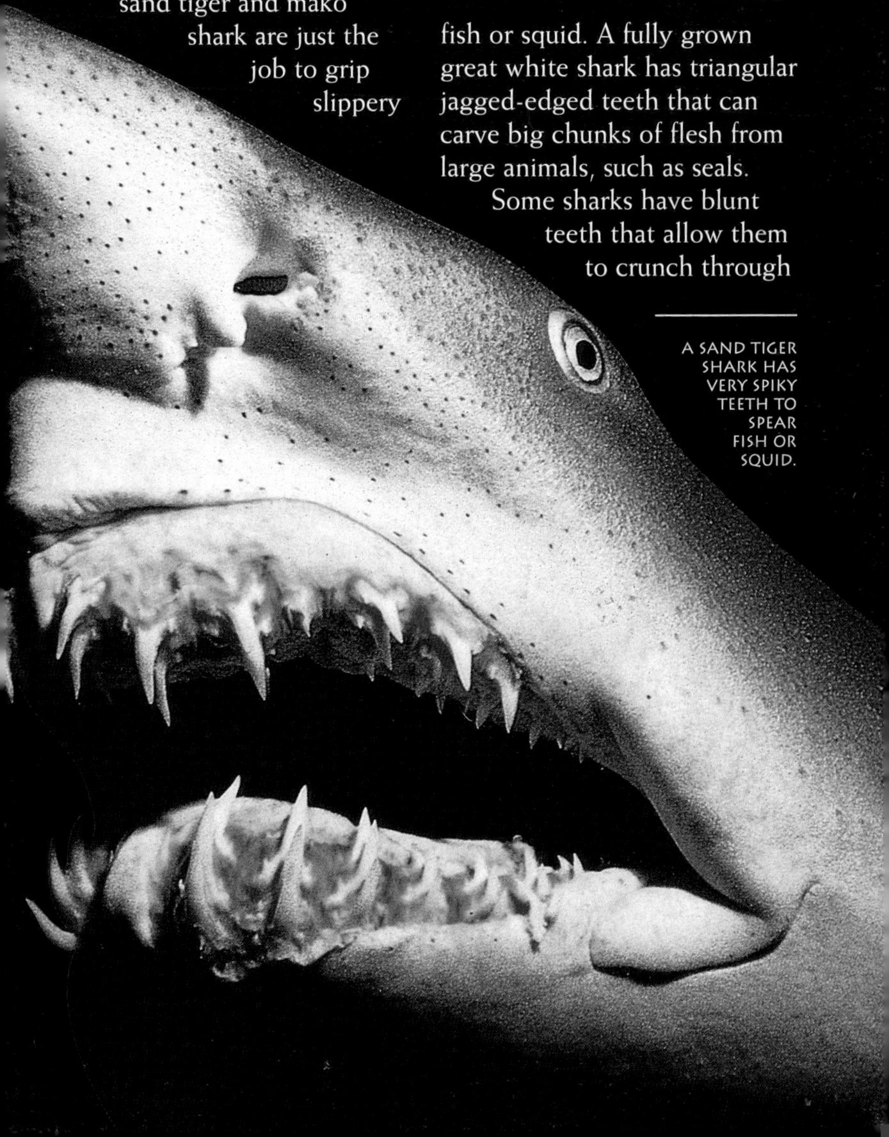

A SAND TIGER SHARK HAS VERY SPIKY TEETH TO SPEAR FISH OR SQUID.

the shells of snails, clams, sea urchins, crabs, and lobsters. The dusky smoothhound shark's blunt teeth are arranged close together for crushing their crab and lobster prey.

M ulti-task teeth
But a few sharks aren't content with single-purpose teeth, and which has three different cutting edges on one tooth. The top of the tooth is pointed, one side has a curved jagged edge, and the other side has sharp toothlets. Equipped with this

THE BIGGEST SHARKS ARE GENTLE FILTER-FEEDERS

might have more than one type in their mouths. For example, the sicklefin weasel shark has curved pointy teeth in the lower jaw to grab octopuses, and jagged-edged teeth in the upper jaw to slice them up.

There are also sharks with different parts to each tooth, such as the tiger shark, type of tooth, the tiger shark can dine on soft foods, such as fish and jellyfish and can also crunch through a turtle's shell. But they're not fussy – tiger sharks are great scavengers and will eat all sorts of things, including dead animals and even rubbish.

WHITE SHARK'S TOOTH

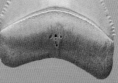

GREAT WHITE SHARK'S TOOTH

TIGER SHARK'S TOOTH

BASKING SHARK'S TEETH

A BASKING SHARK SWIMS WITH ITS MOUTH OPEN TO CATCH PLANKTON.

basking shark's mouth, plankton gets caught in slime on the bristly structures in front of the gills, called gill rakers. Every couple of minutes, the shark shuts its mouth, collapses the gill rakers, and squeezes the whole gooey mass down its throat.

Tiny teeth

Not all sharks have big scary teeth – some no longer need to use theirs at all. The whale shark and basking shark have tiny teeth, especially compared to their gigantic size. They filter small creatures, called plankton, out of the water like a giant sieve. The whale shark sucks in water, while the basking shark swims along with its mouth wide open. Inside the

Jaw action

So that sharks can open their mouths to feed, they need jaws. These are made of tough cartilage, sometimes reinforced with minerals to make the jaw strong enough to crush hard-shelled prey. Large, powerful muscles slam the jaw shut in an instant around helpless prey. The point of each tooth exerts huge pressure, puncturing the

33

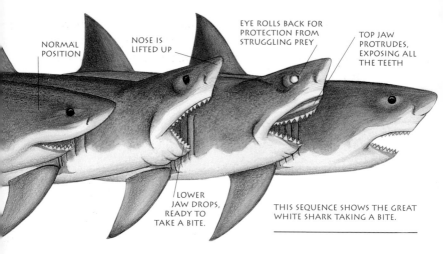

NORMAL
POSITION

NOSE IS
LIFTED UP

EYE ROLLS BACK FOR
PROTECTION FROM
STRUGGLING PREY

TOP JAW
PROTRUDES,
EXPOSING ALL
THE TEETH

LOWER
JAW DROPS,
READY TO
TAKE A BITE.

THIS SEQUENCE SHOWS THE GREAT
WHITE SHARK TAKING A BITE.

skin or shell of the animal it has caught. Unless the shark chooses to let go, it is impossible to wriggle free.

A shark's mouth lies under its head but it can still take a big bite because its upper jaw is only loosely attached to the skull. The shark's upper jaw pushes forward exposing the teeth, and the lower jaw drops. As the upper jaw slams down on prey, the lower jaw moves upwards. Because their jaws push out, sharks can take large

bites without choking, unlike us! However, sharks can't chew their food like we do. When eating large prey, they have to shake their heads from side to side to tear off chunks of flesh.

Great white feeding

One shark that likes to tear off chunks of flesh is the great white. It can grow more than 6 m (20 ft) long, and is the biggest of the hunting sharks. The great white is big enough to eat large prey, such as seals and sea lions. These animals have lots of blubber, or fat, which provides the shark with the energy it needs for swimming fast.

The great white usually approaches its victim from below, charging through the water to take an enormous bite of flesh. If the shark decides

> ### WEIRD WORLD
> THE GREAT WHITE SHARK CAN LIFT ITS HEAD OUT OF THE WATER TO CHECK OUT WHAT IS HAPPENING ON THE SURFACE.

the animal tastes good, it will attack in earnest. A seal may be carried in the shark's mouth as it swims, and then a chunk of its flesh removed. A great white may let go of an injured animal, and then attack it again, until it dies from loss of blood.

hammerhead shark is especially fond of stingrays, and can use its hammer to pin one down while it takes a bite.

Using the head as a clamp works for hammerheads, but thresher sharks use their tails when hunting. The whip-like

A GREAT WHITE ALWAYS HAS AT LEAST 100 FUNCTIONAL TEETH

Heads and tails

Hammerhead sharks don't eat such large prey as the great white. They hunt fish, squid, and other swimming sea creatures. Hammerheads also seek out rays hiding on the sandy sea floor. The great

tail whooshes through the water to herd a shoal of fish. Some fish may be hurt as the tail slaps into them, making easy prey for the thresher.

A GREAT WHITE SHARK LUNGES FOR BAIT, TEETH AND JAWS READY FOR ACTION.

Cookiecutters

The most bizarre feeding technique of all sharks is that of the cookiecutter shark. It is named after the metal cutters used to punch cookie (biscuit) shapes. Its lower jaw is armed with a vicious set of sharp triangular teeth. In comparison to its body size, the teeth of the largetooth cookiecutter are twice the size of a great white's.

The cookiecutter latches onto a large fish or a marine mammal, such as a dolphin,

A CLOSE-UP VIEW OF A COOKIECUTTER MOUTH SHOWS ITS ROW OF SHARP TEETH. IT LEAVES A DISTINCTIVE CIRCULAR WOUND IN ITS PREY.

Nurse shark suction

The nurse shark is too slow to catch fast fish swimming in mid-water. Instead, it prefers to find fish and other animals close to the bottom, or lurking in rocky crevices. The nurse shark sticks its snout into the crevice, and sucks out its prey like an underwater vacuum cleaner. The teeth lie flat in its mouth and point backwards. The means that shelled prey, such as crabs, can be crunched up, and fish cannot escape from the vice-like grip of the shark.

with its sucker-like lips. Digging its teeth deep into the skin, the cookiecutter swivels around to take out a plug of flesh. The telltale sign of a cookiecutter's activities are circular wounds on the sides of the animals they have attacked.

Meal times

That's how sharks capture their prey, but did you realize that sharks hunt at different times? Great white sharks often hunt during the day, when seals and sea lions are most active. Many other sharks prefer to hunt in the limited light of dawn, dusk, or at night. Some sharks hunt in a group, such as the spiny dogfish.

Sharks may gather together if attracted to bait or a large dead animal such as a whale. When this happens, shark senses go into overdrive because of all the blood and food in the water, and they get very excited. Sometimes they attack anything that moves – even some of their pals – in the feeding frenzy.

NURSE AND CARIBBEAN REEF SHARKS CLUSTER AROUND BAIT.

A SURFER SHOWS OFF HIS BOARD AFTER A TIGER SHARK ATTACK.

may bite if it's being fished out of the water, or if a diver is foolish enough to pull its tail for a joke. If a shark thinks that its life is being threatened, it will defend itself.

Unprovoked attacks may occur in murky water or in the surf, where a shark could mistake human feet or limbs for fish. The shark often takes one bite, and then realizes its mistake and swims away. People may need stitches but aren't usually seriously injured.

Scary sharks

But some sharks, particularly the bull shark, tiger shark, and great white, are dangerous and can cause more damage than bad cuts. These big sharks swim close to shore where people swim and surf. Here they can really harm a human, even if they don't intend to.

Bull sharks eat all kinds of different prey, from fish to dolphins. They like shallow

A STREAMLINED FIN SLICES THROUGH THE WATER.

Hungry for humans?

Sharks eat all sorts of different prey but are we on the menu? For most sharks definitely not. Of the few sharks that attack humans, it is usually a case of mistaken identity or because we've invaded their space. Sharks may even swim strangely to warn divers to back off, just as they would do to another shark on their patch. For example, the grey reef shark opens its mouth, arches it back, and lowers its pectoral fins to warn divers away.

Sometimes though, a person may provoke a shark into biting. An irritated shark warm water and tidal creeks – places where they might come across a person. Tiger sharks eat all kinds of things including rubbish. This shows that they are less selective, so may try to eat anything, even people, when they are hungry.

Adult great whites prefer energy-rich fatty food, such as blubber-coated seals and

so the risk of an attack is tiny. But, if you're paddling, swimming, snorkelling, or diving where there could be sharks, it may help to:
• Check with lifeguards, and dive or snorkel instructors about local shark behaviour.

LOG ON...
For more on shark attacks
www.flmnh.ufl.edu/fish/Sharks/sharks.htm

YOU'RE MORE LIKELY TO BE KILLED BY LIGHTNING THAN A SHARK

sea lions to humans. They may attack people surfing near seal colonies because surfers paddling on their boards look like seals to a shark as it swims underneath. Unfortunately, even if a great white doesn't intend to eat a person, one bite can be fatal.

Attacks and safety tips
The International Shark Attack File based in Florida, USA, keeps records of shark attacks. Worldwide there are less than 100 reported attacks on people each year, which result in about ten deaths. You are much more likely to drown, be struck by lightning, or die from a bee sting. Most sharks are shy and keep away from us,

• Make sure you're with other people – sharks are more likely to attack a lone person.
• Avoid being in the water at dawn, dusk, and at night.
• Don't swim if you have an open wound – sharks home in on the smell of blood.
• Don't wear jewellery, as light bouncing off shiny metal might look like the scales of a fish.
• Keep away from places where fish gather, such as in sewage-polluted waters or where people are fishing with baits – sharks could be hunting the fish.
• Don't splash much, and avoid swimming with a splashing dog. Sharks are attracted to the noise.
• Avoid murky water, and wear goggles or a mask so you can see if a shark approaches.

A SHARK IS BORN

Like most animals, male and female sharks get together to produce young. Once the parent sharks court and mate, baby sharks – or pups – develop in three different ways, depending on their species. The first group develop from eggs that their mother has left among seaweed or between rocks. All other sharks grow into pups inside their mother's womb. Of these, one group uses food from their own eggs, and the other group receives food through mum's blood supply – more like mammals than fish!

LOG ON...
For more shark facts and fun
www.kidzone.ws/sharks/

Finding a mate

Before a female shark can become pregnant she must reach an age when she can mate. In most species, this is any time after the age of six. Mating then occurs every year for some species, but probably only every other year for those with long pregnancies.

Sharks often swim great distances to breeding areas. Some, such as the Port Jackson shark, return to the same area each year. But because not many people have seen sharks breeding, no one knows where many go to mate.

But we do know that courtship can be rough for female sharks. Males often swim after females and bite them. Scientists think that this biting may encourage the female to mate.

FEMALE SHARKS HAVE THICK SKINS TO SURVIVE COURTSHIP BITES

With large sharks, the male needs to grab hold of the female to mate. As sharks haven't got limbs, he has to bite her pectoral fin to hang onto her. For this reason, the female blue shark's skin is three times thicker than the male's!

Competing for a mate

For smaller, more flexible sharks, mating is a lot easier. The male can wrap his body around the female instead of biting her. For example, the male lesser spotted dogfish

DURING COURTSHIP, THE MALE WHITETIP REEF SHARK BITES THE FIN OF THE FEMALE.

41

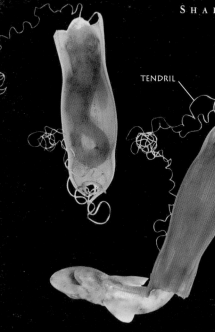

TENDRIL

A YOUNG DOGFISH GROWS INSIDE AN EGG BEFORE HATCHING.

Mating sharks

Once the sharks have courted, they mate. This is very different from bony fish, who simply shed sperm and eggs into the water. Instead, a male shark has to place sperm inside the female's body. He does this using one of the two claspers that lie under his body between the pelvic fins. He rotates one clasper forward, and then flushes sperm into the female's cloaca – a body opening under her belly. The sperm then fertilize the female's eggs, although some sharks can store the sperm and fertilize their eggs later.

Once the eggs are fertilized, they start to develop inside the female. This is when things start to become different between the species of shark, depending on how the pups develop.

can curl his body around the female. But first he has to "win" her – and there is a lot of competition among the male dogfish. Sometimes a female may even need to seek refuge in a cave to escape from all the attention.

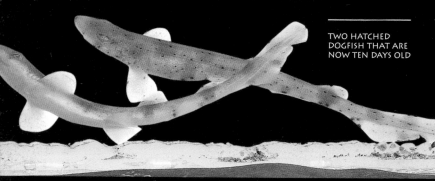

TWO HATCHED DOGFISH THAT ARE NOW TEN DAYS OLD

Shark eggs

A few types of shark lay eggs into the water after they are fertilized. They only lay a few large eggs, unlike bony fish who shed thousands of tiny ones. The eggs have tough horny coats, called mermaid's purses, to help protect them. Dogfish eggs have long curly bits, called tendrils, which wind around seaweed so they're not washed away. Bamboo, epaulette,

temperature, the baby shark breaks free of its egg nursery, and begins its life in the ocean.

In the womb

Most sharks don't lay eggs. Instead, they give birth to fully formed little sharks, called pups. There are two ways that the pups grow inside their mother, depending on the type of shark. In some sharks, the embryos feed on the yolk attached to their bellies.

A PREGNANT BLACKTIP SHARK SWIMS IN THE ATLANTIC OCEAN.

and zebra sharks lay eggs with tufts of sticky, hair-like fibres that anchor them to coral and rocky reefs.

Apart from laying her eggs in the safest place possible, the mother shark does nothing more for her babies, and the father shark is long gone.

When this is used up, they get extra nutrients from fluid secreted into the womb or they eat unfertilized eggs.

The first pup to hatch inside the sand tiger shark devours some brothers and sisters as

Growing inside

Once the eggs are laid, the baby shark, or embryo, inside develops, feeding on the nutrient-rich yolk attached to its belly. From several weeks to 15 months later, depending on the shark and the water

WEIRD WORLD
FEMALE HORN SHARKS LAY SOFT, SPIRAL-SHAPED EGGS, WHICH THEY PUSH INTO CREVICES. AS THEY HARDEN THE EGGS BECOME SAFELY WEDGED AND HIDDEN FROM VIEW.

hatched embryos, and then feeds on the unfertilized eggs. Finally, only two pups are left – one on each side of the mother's womb. By feasting on their siblings, sand tiger pups grow large, and are more likely to survive once they're born.

Cord connection
The other way pups grow inside their mother occurs in sharks such as hammerheads and lemon sharks. Instead of depending on the yolk for food, the embryos tap into the womb like human babies. Each growing shark – and there can be many – has an umbilical cord that connects it to its mother's blood supply. Blood vessels in the cord bring food and oxygen to each baby, and take away its wastes.

Pregnant mums
As well as the two different ways baby

sharks grow inside their mums, there is also a variation in the length of time the female shark is pregnant. The bonnethead shark has a short pregnancy lasting only a few months. But most sharks have a pregnancy of at least nine months, the same as human mothers. The spiny dogfish has about a 22-month pregnancy – that's the same as an elephant – and then gives birth to between ten and 20 pups. Basking shark mums are pregnant for more than two years.

Giving birth
When the time comes to give birth, the female shark generally loses her appetite. This is so she won't be tempted to eat her own pups! She also

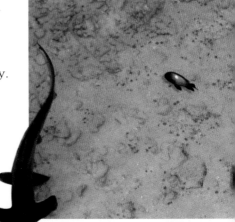

keeps away from males to avoid the risk of them eating her newborn pups.

Lemon sharks give birth in shallow water in sheltered lagoons where larger sharks cannot reach them. The pups are born tail-first, and soon swim off into the sea to fend for themselves.

The bigger the pup when it is born, the better its chance of survival. The sand tiger, dusky shark, and great white shark's pups are about 1 m (3.3 ft) long at birth, already too big for most predators. Lemon shark pups are about 60 cm (2 ft) at birth so must hide away in the safety of mangrove roots

SHARKS ARE BORN READY TO FEED AND SURVIVE ON THEIR OWN

Hammerhead sharks also give birth to pups. Fortunately, their heads are reasonably soft so they do not get jammed in the mother's birth canal. Once born, the pups must find food and escape predators all on their own.

to avoid being eaten by other sharks. Whale shark pups are also born 60 cm (2 ft) long – they have a lot of growing to do before they deserve the title of the biggest fish in the sea!

Sharks grow slowly all their lives and it may be a few years until they are ready to have pups of their own. If they're not caught by people or weakened by disease, they can live to a grand old age – even as old as 70!

HAMMERHEAD PUPS SWIM WITH FISH IN SHALLOW WATER NEAR OAHU, HAWAII.

COUSIN RAY

Sharks get a lot of attention from us, perhaps because they're scary. Some of their close relatives are worth finding out about too. Rays and chimaeras are closely related to sharks and are just as intriguing. They have enough similarities – specifically a cartilage skeleton – to be cousins, but plenty of differences too. This side of the family is generally harmless, although some species can give a nasty sting or vicious shock!

Spot the difference

At first glance, most rays don't look anything like sharks. But a closer look shows they are, in fact, flat sharks with long tails. Just like sharks, they have skeletons made of flexible cartilage. Also, they would sink if they stopped swimming, because they don't have a gas-filled swim bladder like bony fish. So in some ways they are very like sharks.

But, there are lots of differences too. Unlike sharks, most rays rest on the sea floor. For this reason, their eyes sit on top of their heads, as there is not much point in looking at sand all the time. They are more interested in keeping watch for predators!

LOG ON...
www.aqua.org/animals/species/prrays.html

A SOUTHERN STINGRAY SWIMS IN THE CARIBBEAN SEA.

WEIRD WORLD

RAYS EVOLVED FROM SHARKS ABOUT 200 MILLION YEARS AGO. THE EARLIEST KNOWN RAYS LOOKED LIKE SHARKS, AND FOSSILS SHOW THAT SOME WERE SIMILAR TO MODERN GUITARFISH.

47

In order to breathe, a ray usually takes water in through a large spiracle, or hole, behind each eye. This is just as well, because a ray's mouth faces the sand, and taking in water the usual way could mean getting a sandy mouthful! Water is then passed over the gills, and flows out through gill slits, which are under the ray's flat head – not on its side like a shark.

Swimming along

The biggest difference between sharks and rays is the ray's huge pectoral fins. These extend in a continuous sweep along each side of the head and down the body. Most rays swim by rippling the edges of their pectoral fins in a wave that passes from the front to the back of the fins, propelling the ray forward.

Rays usually have spindly tails that are not much use for swimming. One exception is the electric ray with its thicker tail that swishes from side to side to help it swim.

Highly mobile

The eagle and cownose rays are good swimmers. In these rays, their pointed

A SPOTTED RAY RIPPLES ITS PECTORAL FINS TO SWIM.

pectoral fins are like wings that beat up and down so they seem to fly through the water. By beating their fins alternately they can turn this way and that to escape hungry sharks.

Manta rays have the biggest wings of all. They can grow to more than 6 m (20 ft) across – that's bigger than a car! These rays are famous for

leaping clear out of the water.
No one knows why mantas
leap but it could be to help
them remove parasites from
their skin.

estuaries.
River rays
always live in
freshwater, as you
can guess by their name.

Where rays live

There are about 600 species
of ray, most of which live in
the sea. They can be found in
all oceans, from shallow water
to depths of nearly 3 km
(1.8 miles), and most live on
or close to the sea floor. The
deepest dwellers are members
of the skate family, which are
typical rays with diamond
or round-shaped bodies and
slender tails. Some rays, such
as stingarees, venture into

Finding food

Most rays feed along the sea
floor, which is not surprising
since their mouths lie under
their heads. Like sharks, they
have electrosense pores that
can help them find hidden
food. Once they've located
their prey, they capture it
in different ways. Eagle rays
squeeze their pectoral fins
together to pop clams out
of mud. Cownose rays also use
their pectoral fins to clear away

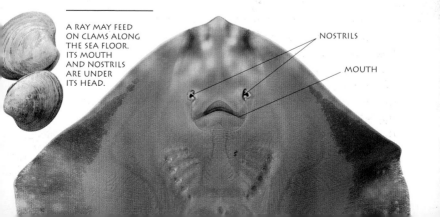

A RAY MAY FEED
ON CLAMS ALONG
THE SEA FLOOR.
ITS MOUTH
AND NOSTRILS
ARE UNDER
ITS HEAD.

NOSTRILS

MOUTH

sand from a
clam or a crab.
The shellfish
is cracked
open by bands
of flat, crushing
teeth in the ray's
mouth. Only the juicier
morsels are swallowed.

Shock tactics

Electric rays feed on fish
and other creatures lurking on,
or near, the sea floor. They live
in warm or cool coastal waters.
Once in contact with

their
prey, they
stun it with
powerful electric shocks.
Electricity is generated in large
muscles on either side of their
disc-shaped bodies. The blocks
of muscles are like a series
of batteries linked together,
and are capable of packing
a powerful shock! The stunned
prey is then fanned into the

ray's mouth by the pectoral
fins. Electricity works for
defence too. If you stepped
on an electric ray, you'd
certainly feel the shock!

Filter feeders

Not all rays are this scary.
Mantas have tiny teeth and
filter-feed plankton from the
water, just like whale and
basking sharks. Mantas
have large lobes on
their heads to guide
a steady stream
of plankton into
their gigantic
mouths as they
swim along.
Mantas may
swim together

in big circles
through patches
of food-rich water.

Social lives

Other rays also congregate
where food is good. Cownose

rays often swim together,
making daily journeys inshore
to feed in sandy or muddy
shallows. Rays also group
together to mate, and most

COWNOSE RAYS SWIM
IN A GROUP NEAR THE
GALAPAGOS ISLANDS.

Sting in the tail

Whether busy being
sociable, looking for food,
or resting on the sea floor –
rays can be at risk from attack.
To protect themselves, some
have large prickles that run
along their back and tail as
a body armour. Stingrays have
a long whip-like tail, which is
armed with one or more spines.

give birth to a small number
of pups. However, skates lay
large eggs with long curly
tendrils that anchor each
one to the sea floor.

If a stingray is stepped on or attacked it whips its tail around to impale its spines into the flesh of the intruder. The spines as the southern stingray, are actually friendly, curious creatures that approach divers to find out what's going on.

SAWFISH LIVE IN RIVERS AND LAKES, AS WELL AS IN THE SEA

can get lodged in the flesh, which is painful enough. But the spines are also loaded with venom that produces a bad reaction, and can make a person feel sick or worse. Stingrays only use their weapons if provoked. Some, such

Chainsaw massacre
Sawfish are not as friendly. These types of ray have a weapon at their front end. The huge snout is equipped with sharp teeth on

each side. If a sawfish is caught in a fishing net, it can lash out and wound anyone within range. It slashes at fish with its saw to stun or kill them.

Sawfish have look-a-like shark relatives – the sawsharks. They also have a saw on their snouts. So how can you tell a sawfish from a sawshark? Take

A SAWFISH DISPLAYS
ITS FRIGHTENING
TEETH-LINED SNOUT.

a good look at the sharp end –
if you dare! Sawsharks have
a pair of feelers, called barbels,
half way along the snout.
They also have gill slits on
the sides of the head, instead
of underneath, like sawfish.

Guitarfish

Other shark-like rays are the
guitarfish, which live in
warm coastal
waters to
depths
of a few
hundred metres.
As you can guess,
they look like a musical
instrument with a roundish
body, and a broader tail than
most rays. The ones with the
broadest tails swim like sharks
by sweeping the tail back and
forth, while fins on their back
act as stabilizers.

Distant cousins

More distant cousins of sharks
and rays are chimaeras. On the
outside chimaeras look nothing
like sharks or rays. They have
smooth skins, big eyes, and big
heads. The first fin on the back
can be raised and lowered, and
a flap covers their gills, as if
they are bony fish. It's their
cartilage skeleton that unites
them with sharks and rays.

For defence, chimaeras have
a venomous spine on their
backs. Most chimaeras prefer
deep cold water but can be
found in the shallows if it
is cold enough. There
are many
different
chimaeras –
the plownoses
have a hooked snout for
probing the sea floor for food,
while those with long tails like
rats go by the name of ratfish.

Sharks certainly have some
interesting relatives whether it's
the odd-looking chimaeras or
the curious, but scary, stingray.
For most it is hard to tell they
are related but if you looked
inside every shark, ray, or
chimaera, you'd find that
rubbery skeleton of cartilage.

A PLOWNOSE CHIMAERA
SWIMS OFF THE COAST
OF NEW ZEALAND.

VILE VENOM

Sharks and their relatives are not the only scary creatures in the sea. Other types of fish can also be harmful. Sea creatures may use venom – a poison that is jabbed into the skin by spines, fangs, or teeth – as a way to subdue their prey or to defend themselves. Some other fish protect themselves by coating their bodies in poisonous slime so that a predator will spit them out. If we handle or step on these creatures they will treat us as enemies.

THIS VENOMOUS SCORPIONFISH IS DISGUISED BY ITS WEED-LIKE APPEARANCE.

Stinging fish

You've just seen that stingrays have one or more spines loaded with venom on their tail. Some bony fish, like the scorpionfish, are also equipped to sting. Their stings aren't in their tail, they're on their fins instead. The fin that runs along the back of the fish has the most.

Why do scorpionfish need their venom? Most scorpionfish spend their time lying on rocks or corals waiting to pounce on a fish or crab wandering by. As they lie in wait, a larger fish could easily attack them.

So, they need good protection. Their first line of defence is camouflage – they look like weed-covered rocks or corals. This disguise keeps them hidden from predators and their prey. If they were brightly coloured, they'd probably starve to death, as their prey would see them and quickly swim away!

A scorpionfish's venomous spines

are its second line of defence. At the base of each spine is a sack of venom. If bitten by a predator the venom is squeezed out as the spines penetrate the predator's skin, injecting it with poison. The problem for people is that the scorpionfish, and some of their relatives such as the stonefish, have such good disguises that we can't see them, and might step on their spines.

Stripy lionfish

The most elegant members of the scorpionfish family are the lionfish. They have long venomous spines on their backs that give

them excellent protection from predators. At night, they hover around coral reefs feeding on small creatures. During the day, lionfish often hide in caves or under coral ledges, where they hardly move at all. When they swim out from a coral reef,

A LIONFISH DISPLAYS THE VENOMOUS SPINES ON ITS BACK AS IT HUNTS FOR FOOD.

their stripes stand out and serve as a bright warning to predators to keep away! For this reason, they are fearless creatures, and divers can swim very close to them.

Poison and prickles

Porcupinefish are other creatures armed with spines on their body. In some species, the spines stick out permanently, but in others the spines lie flat against the body unless under attack. When attacked they inflate into a spiny ball by swallowing lots of water. A fish or seal trying to eat an inflated porcupinefish will find it difficult to get its jaws around the spiky, balloon-like body.

Prickly pufferfish, as their names implies, can inflate. Some of them have another trick too – they coat their skin with poisonous slime. Worse still, many pufferfish have a strong poison in their liver and gut that affects the nervous system of people who might eat them.

Incredibly, the flesh from some pufferfish is a delicacy in Japan. The flesh, called fugu, is served at special restaurants where the chefs perform the delicate task of cutting out the most poisonous bits. You would have to trust the chef to eat there!

Spiny skins

People do like eating strange seafood – even sea urchins! Their roes (eggs) are a delicacy in Japan, France, and Spain. Unfortunately, its coat of needle-sharp spines does little to protect the urchin from

A CHEF PREPARES FUGU. FIRST, HE REMOVES THE POISONOUS PARTS OF THE PUFFERFISH!

LOG ON...
www.aloha.com/
~lifeguards/critters.html

humans intent on eating it.

Some urchins can be dangerous to pick up. Grab a black urchin from the Mediterranean Sea and its spines would puncture your skin. Stepping on one would be even worse as the needles can break off in your skin and are hard to remove.

The tropical long-spined urchin is even better equipped, with poison-coated spines longer than a man's hand. Some creatures have worked out a sneaky way to prey on these urchins. The triggerfish blows water at the urchin to flip it over. It then bites the underneath, where there are fewer spines.

Long-spined urchins provide a safe refuge for other creatures who know their predators won't come near the spines. Razorfish hang about head-down among the spines, their vertical stripes blending in nicely.

Blue for danger

Another venomous sea creature is the blue-ringed octopus. It is only the size of a person's hand but its poison is very powerful indeed.

Each octopus contains enough venom to paralyze ten people!

The blue-ringed octopus lives in rock pools along the Australian coast and, like all octopuses, has a parrot-like beak. As it bites into prey with its beak, the wound can be flooded with venom. When provoked, the blue rings on its tentacles and body flash more brightly. A clear signal that means leave me alone!

———————

A BLUE-RINGED OCTOPUS HAS A BEAK THAT CAN INJECT POWERFUL VENOM.

Colourful cones

Cone snails are also venomous sea creatures. They have beautifully patterned shells, although you should never touch them or take them from a reef. Sea creatures should avoid getting close too! Cone snails have dart-like hollow teeth, which they jab into their prey. The teeth come loaded with venom, which is so potent that the cone snail can paralyze prey that is larger than itself. The poison affects the prey quickly and it cannot swim away. It is then engulfed by the cone snail's expandable food tube and gobbled up.

Cone snails that feed on fish have stronger venom than those that eat worms or other snails. A few fish-eating cone snails, like the geography cone, can kill people with their venom.

Sea snakes

Of all the venomous creatures in the world, we often think of snakes when it comes to deadly bites. Those that live in the sea have some of the most toxic venom of any snake. The poison is injected through sharp, curved teeth at the front of the sea snake's mouth. As the snake strikes, the venom passes through the hollow fangs and into the wound of the victim.

Sea snakes live in the tropical waters of the Pacific and Indian oceans where they feed on fish. Most sea snakes grow to about 0.5–1 m (1.5–3.3 ft) in length, although some can reach 2 m (6.6 ft). They power along with the help of their paddle-like tail. Sea snakes can dive to more than 50 m (160 ft) and can stay underwater for several hours on one lungful of air, and by absorbing oxygen from the water through their skin.

It must be unnerving for a diver to be inspected by a curious sea snake as it swims past! Despite their reputation, however, people are rarely injured by sea snakes.

Whether armed with fangs or spines, sea creatures have to make the best of their weapons to survive in the oceans.

SEA SNAKES CAN CLOSE THEIR NOSTRILS TO KEEP WATER OUT

A BANDED SEA SNAKE SLITHERS OVER A REEF OFF THE PHILIPPINE ISLANDS.

STINGING JELLIES

Jellyfish may look beautiful as they slowly swim along, but beware! Their tentacles are armed with thousands of deadly stings. Jellyfish aren't the only stingers in the sea – their relatives, such as corals, sea anemones, and sea firs are also armed. Jellyfish stun or paralyze prey with their stings, which are key to their survival as an important ocean predator.

Swimming bells

Jellyfish have simple bell-shaped bodies made of a squishy substance like jelly – which is how they got their name. They range in colour from yellowish orange to pinkish purple. Deep-sea jellyfish can even glow in the dark when disturbed.

To swim, the jellyfish contracts its bell so that water whooshes out and propels the jellyfish along. The bell then springs back into shape and water rushes back inside ready for the next contraction. Jellyfish are not strong swimmers so are often swept along by currents.

No brain

Jellyfish don't have brains but they do fine without them. A network of nerves sends signals around the bell so the jellyfish can coordinate its movements.

On the rim of the bell, gravity receptors tell the jellyfish which way up it is facing, while light receptors let the jellyfish know how far it is from the sunlit surface.

Stinging tentacles

As the jellyfish swims along, the tentacles, armed with thousands of tiny stinging cells, trail behind. Each cell is usually equipped with a trigger that is set off by the touch and smell of a passing fish or shrimp. When this happens, the cell turns inside out – like blowing out the end of a rubber glove. As it does so, it shoots out a minute, thread-like tube, which twirls around to cut into the flesh of the victim. The tube injects venom into the prey, and, when hit by many stings, the prey is stunned or paralyzed. Other cells on the tentacles are sticky or coil around parts of

WEIRD WORLD

DESPITE THEIR NAME, JELLYFISH ARE NOT ACTUALLY FISH. THEY'RE CNIDARIANS – SIMPLE CREATURES WITH STINGING CELLS. JELLYFISH ARE 95 PER CENT WATER – THEY HAVE NO HEART, BLOOD, BONES, OR BRAIN!

the prey to make sure it doesn't get away after being stung.

Eating prey

Once the prey is stunned and captured, the jellyfish uses its frilly arms to pass the creature up to its mouth. In some types of jellyfish, the tentacles retract, as though they are on a winch, bringing the prey towards the mouth. Digestive juices break down the food into a soupy

SEA NETTLES, A TYPE OF JELLYFISH, SWIM OFF THE WEST COAST OF THE USA.

LOG ON...
www.aqua.org/
animals/species/jellies.html

mass, which is absorbed by the cells in the bell. Indigestible bits are dumped out through the same opening. Jellyfish only have one body opening for eating and excreting. Yuck!

Dangerous jellies

Jellyfish mostly use their stings to catch prey, but people can also get stung if they touch one or swim into a trailing tentacle. Not all jellyfish have powerful stings. For example, the moon jellyfish uses slime to trap its food, so only needs a weak sting.

Jellyfish that swarm in coastal waters are hard to avoid. People often name these stingers after living things that sting us on land, such as nettles or wasps.

The most deadly jellyfish – the box jellyfish – has a short, simple name that diguises its nasty nature. It lives in warm coastal waters off northern Australia and south-east Asia. Its bunches of long tentacles trail behind it for up to 3 m (10 ft), and its bell is the size of a person's head. The box jellyfish is virtually see-through so it is hard to spot in the water.

Jellyfish season

To avoid being stung, people are advised not to swim in summer when box jellyfish swarm in coastal waters. Signs at the beach warn bathers not to enter the water. Anyone

THIS BOX JELLYFISH MODEL SHOWS A CLOSE UP OF THE DEADLY STINGING CELLS IN ITS TENTACLES.

AS THE STINGING CELL SENSES A FISH BRUSHING PAST, IT SHOOTS OUT A BARBED TUBE.

THE BARB CUTS INTO THE FISH'S FLESH.

VENOM IS INJECTED INTO THE FISH.

CORAL, SUCH AS THIS PIPE-ORGAN CORAL, STINGS AND CATCHES PLANKTON IN ITS TINY TENTACLES.

A settled life

The Portuguese-man-of-war spends its life adrift in warm waters. Their cousins, the sea

MAN-OF-WAR TENTACLES CAN BE AS LONG AS A BLUE WHALE

who gets too close to the box jellyfish will find themselves under attack! Tentacles stick to the skin and are hard to remove without triggering more stings. They are incredibly painful and leave nasty red marks.

Men-at-war

A distant relative of the box jellyfish, the Portuguese-man-of-war, delivers stings that are so painful you could faint! English sailors named it after the old Portuguese fighting ship – the man-of-war – because the colony's float looked like the ship's triangular sail. This float sits up out of the water keeping the jellyfish afloat, like a balloon. Its long tentacles, which are equipped with nasty stings, find food and defend the colony. The tentacles also haul food up into little stomachs where it is digested. Other parts of the jellyfish devote themselves to making sperm or eggs.

firs, grow anchored to surfaces – anything from rocks to piers. They have a bunch of flower-like heads each circled by a ring of stinging tentacles.

Sea anemones also like a settled life although they can creep along on their base. Some even do somersaults to escape being eaten! Like all their relatives, they have stinging tentacles to capture food. Some types of tropical anemone can give a nasty sting.

Coral reef

Unlike squishy jellyfish and sea anemones, corals have hard, stony skeletons. It is their skeletons that help make coral reefs – home for many sea creatures. Look closely at a coral and you will see that its tiny colony members resemble mini sea anemones. They get some of their food by capturing plankton in their stinging tentacles. Corals also have tiny plant-like cells inside their tissues that make food using the energy from sunlight.

Friends and enemies

Surprisingly, despite their powerful stings, jellyfish and anemones also provide a home for fish. For example, the splendid tentacles of the lion's mane jellyfish shelter young fish. The fish seem to be rarely stung and are safe from larger predators.

Some fish don't seem to be affected when they nibble at an anemone's tentacles.

The beautiful clownfish shelter in large anemones, and secrete a thick layer of slime that stops the anemone's stinging cells from firing.

Jellyfish and their relatives may be simple forms of life but they have been adrift in the ocean for 600 million years. Stinging tentacles have proved to be just as good a way to catch prey as rows and rows of sharp teeth.

CLOWNFISH SWIM SAFELY AMONG STINGING ANEMONES.

NASTY NIPPERS

Crunch! That's the sound you would hear as a crab, lobster, mantis shrimp, or other crustacean – an animal with a tough, crusty, outer shell – clamps its menacing claws around prey. People can also get a nasty nip – especially if the crab or lobster feels threatened. Their pincers, or claws, have sharp edges which make them powerful weapons.

Crunching claws

The biggest claws belong to some of the largest crustaceans – the lobster. The giants of the lobster world grow to about 1 m (3.3 ft) long and have two huge claws at the front. The claws are not identical.

One claw – the lobster's crusher – has a knobbly edge like a nutcracker which is used for crushing hard-shelled prey. The other claw, the cutter, has sharp blades like scissors. The lobster uses it for snipping up

LOG ON...
www.aqua.org/animals/
species/bluecrab.htm1

soft creatures or dead flesh. Inside, large muscles operate the claws, allowing the lobster to grab prey and cut it up.

Facing a challenge

Lobsters lurk under rocky ledges with their claws facing out, ready to challenge intruders. At night they venture out over the sea floor finding dead or dying animals to feed on. If enemies approach, they can flap their tails to swim backwards. A cornered lobster puts up a good fight, brandishing its claws to show it is well armed. If that doesn't work, the lobster will try to nip the attacker.

Smashing claws

The record for the "fastest claw in the sea" goes to the mantis shrimps. Mantis shrimps shoot out their front claws in a fraction of a second. Some have spiny claws that spear fish and soft prey. Others have club-shaped claws for smashing shelled prey to bits. These mantis shrimps can even break the toughened glass of an aquarium!

Mantis shrimps generally live in warmer waters where they lurk in burrows which they have dug out of the sand, mud, or shell material on the sea floor. Fishers that have dredged up these little monsters can get a slashed finger or thumb as they try to get them out of their nets.

Scuttle and swim

Another crusty sea creature with sharp nippers is the crab. Some are good swimmers, with flat, paddle-like back legs. Their other legs are used to scuttle along the sea floor.

The blue crab lives in bays and estuaries along the east

THE COMMON LOBSTER RESTS IN A ROCKY CREVICE. IF AN ENEMY APPROACHES, THE LOBSTER WAVES ITS PINCERS AS A THREAT.

coast of North America.
It is a versatile swimmer that
can reach speeds of up to 1 m
(3.3 ft) per second. It can swim
sideways, backwards, forwards,
and can even hover. Usually,
it buries itself in the mud and
grabs a fish swimming by with
its long vicious-looking claws.

New shells

Like all crabs and their
relatives, blue crabs have to
shed, or moult, their shells as
they outgrow them. The old
shell breaks off and makes way
for a new one that takes a few
days to harden. During this
time, the crab is an easy
target for predators.

Some crabs, such as the
hermit crab, need more
protection because their
abdomens stay soft all the
time. So, to protect

itself the hermit crab lives
inside an empty sea snail's
shell. One claw is bigger than
the other and is used to block
up the entrance of the shell –
just like a front door. When a
hermit crab grows bigger, it has
to move home. First, it finds a
bigger shell. Then it carefully
measures the dimensions by
feeling inside the shell with
its claws, before moving in.

Protection and camouflage

Hermit crabs like having
guests. They put sea
anemones on their shells
to help ward off

predators. A fish trying to devour a hermit crab may get a mouthful of stings instead. The anemone benefits too by feeding on particles of food that the crab drops.

While some hermit crabs have anemone friends, sponge crabs like sponges. Not that sponges can sting but they do help the crab hide from enemies such as large fish and sharks. The crab uses its claws to snip the sponge into just the right shape to cover its body.

WEIRD WORLD
CRABS USE THEIR CLAWS TO SIGNAL TO POTENTIAL MATES DURING COURTSHIP. THE MALE FIDDLER CRAB ATTRACTS A FEMALE INTO HIS BURROW BY WAVING A CLAW.

Others, such as the decorator crab, put bits of seaweed on their shells, hoping they will grow to give them camouflage.

Claws are handy tools and good weapons for crustaceans. Their crusty shell is useful as armour – but it has a drawback. It has to be shed as it grows leaving the lobster, mantis shrimp, or crab vulnerable until the new shell hardens.

A BLUE CRAB WITH CLAWS READY TO GRAB A FISH AS IT SWIMS PAST.

MONSTERS OF THE DEEP

DRAGONFISH LIVE IN THE OCEAN DEPTHS.

The sea has always inspired myth and mystery. For centuries, little was known of its depths or the strange creatures that lived there, and frightening encounters with bizarre sea beasts led to far-fetched stories. Today, there is still much of the deep sea to explore and lots more to discover about sharks and other sea creatures.

Shark stories

People like stories about sharks whether they've met one or not. Such is their influence that traditional stories from Pacific Islanders' tell of sea gods that could magically change from a person into a shark and back again. In some Pacific cultures, boys had to catch sharks as part of their rite of passage into manhood.

Today, blockbuster movies really grab our attention.

Jaws, the movie made in 1975, is a classic thriller about a rogue great white shark intent on eating people. A scary, but invented, story!

S ea serpents

Among the favourite monsters of old were sea serpents. These a flaming crimson fin on its back, and long fin rays on top of its head. The oarfish is rarely seen as it usually lives at great depths down in the ocean. It feeds on plankton

LOG ON...
www.seasky.org/
monsters/sea7a1.html

SAILORS INVENTED SEA SERPENT TALES TO ACCOUNT FOR LOST SHIPS

dragon-like monsters were shown in paintings and talked about in sailors' stories. But could a real creature have given rise to these legendary beasts?

A likely candidate is the oarfish which boasts a silvery, ribbon-like body more than 10 m (33 ft) long. It has so it is hardly a monster!

Another possible source of inspiration for sea serpents is the frilled shark. This shark has a long body, a snake-like mouth, and rarely comes to the

A SEA SERPENT OR A FAKE? THIS PHOTO WAS TAKEN IN THE USA, IN 1906.

THE ANGLERFISH
HAS SHARP TEETH
AND A LUMINOUS
LURE TO ATTRACT PREY
IN THE DARK DEPTHS.

surface. Unusually, the frilled shark has six pairs of frilly-edged gill slits, and these give the shark its name. Seafarers may have seen this shark for many years before scientists studied it in the late 1800s. Corpses of basking sharks have certainly been mistaken for sea serpents.

THIS HATCHET FISH MODEL SHOWS IT HAS LARGE EYES TO SEEE IN THE GLOOM.

Tentacle tales

When it comes to monsters, those with lots of legs can be scary! Think of octopuses and squid, then imagine them the size of a ship. Hey presto, you have a corker of a monster. The kraken, a creature from Norwegian mythology, was just such a monster. Some drawings show the kraken with eight legs like an octopus.

As far as real octopuses go, the giant octopus from the north Pacific Ocean is the biggest. It grows to nearly 10 m (33 ft) across, from tentacle tip to tentacle tip. If touched, the giant octopus may give a diver a friendly embrace, but it is unlikely to do much more than pull out a diver's mouthpiece.

Giant squid

It is more likely that a giant squid was mistaken for being the kraken. The giant squid is big, VERY big, growing up to 18 m (60 ft) long. It also has the biggest eyeballs of any living creature!

No giant squid has been seen or filmed alive in its deep home – yet! Film crews have even tried placing cameras on sperm whales (who hunt giant squid) without success. We know they exist though, because they've been found dead on the beach or in the stomachs of sperm whales.

Monsters in the deep

Deep-sea fish fit the role of scary monsters perfectly because they look so weird. They have evil-looking, gaping jaws, equipped with dagger-like teeth. They have appropriate names like dragonfish, hatchet fish, or anglerfish. There is not much food in the dark, cold depths. So, when a meal does come along, having a big jaw means they can swallow a creature that is larger than themselves.

KRONOSAURUS, A TYPE OF PLIOSAUR, LIVED IN THE OCEANS ABOUT 100 MILLION YEARS AGO. IT HAD A LONG BODY AND BIG, SHARP TEETH.

Lights in the dark

Then there are the strangely named rat-trap fish. Of course they don't trap rats, but the lower jaw is armed with long fangs and opens wide enough to chomp down on prey the same size as itself. These fish have their own "torch" – a light organ below each eye. This shines a red light that helps them find prey.

Megatooth

Some of the scariest sea monsters ever are no longer with us – they're extinct. So there's no chance you'll meet one! Among the extinct sharks, the most alarming is the megalodon, or megatooth shark as some like to call it. Scientists have found fossils of their teeth that show a megalodon's tooth is at least twice the size of a great white's. Now think of rows and rows of these teeth, and a huge set of jaws, and that's scary!

The megalodon is only known from its teeth and vertebrae. Scientists still debate whether it is a relative of the great white or not. We do know, however, that megalodon ate whales because fossil whale bones have been found with saw-marks that fit the serrated pattern of megalodon teeth. Luckily for us, megalodon became extinct two million years ago.

WEIRD WORLD

ONE TYPE OF PLESIOSAUR – KNOWN AS A CRYPTOCLIDUS – USED TO SWALLOW STONES TO REDUCE ITS NATURAL BUOYANCY. THIS ALLOWED THE CREATURES TO MAKE DEEP DIVES IN PURSUIT OF PREY.

Giant sea reptiles

The last of the giant sea reptiles disappeared about 65 million years ago – at the same time as the dinosaurs became extinct on land. The biggest of these sea reptiles were the pliosaurs. These hefty beasts paddled through the ocean, hunting other sea creatures. Pliosaurs had

If there were plesiosaurs in the depths of Loch Ness they'd have to surface for air. So why is the monster so rarely seen?

Sea monsters, whether based on reality or not, are just good fun. Searching for the truth

THE BIGGEST KRONOSAURUS TEETH WERE 25 CM (10 IN) LONG

enormous jaws lined with sharp teeth, so took big chunks out of their prey.

Loch Ness or not?
Slender-necked plesiosaurs also paddled about the sea. Some could twirl their necks to grab fish in their jaws. Plesiosaurs are one source of inspiration for the Loch Ness monster, reputed to live in a deep lake (loch) in Scotland. In the 1930s, a fake head, looking much like that of a plesiosaur, was photographed as a hoax in Loch Ness.

about monsters can inspire us to look further into the untold mysteries of the sea.

A FOSSIL MEGALODON'S TOOTH (ACTUAL SIZE) IS AT LEAST TWICE THE SIZE OF A GREAT WHITE'S.

OCEANS AT RISK

The world's oceans are teeming with life – from top predator sharks to the tiny plankton that drift on the surface. All of these sea creatures form part of a chain of feeding links – made up of predators and prey – known as a food chain. If human activities, such as overfishing, upset this delicate balance then the ocean is put at risk. But there are things we can do to help.

Sharks at the top
Scary or not, sharks help maintain the balance of life in the sea. They have an important position as top predators in the food chain.

If the number of sharks is reduced then this has a knock-on effect all the way through the feeding links. Sharks keep the numbers of large fish

SHARKS EAT LARGE FISH, SUCH AS COD.

BIG SHARKS ARE AT THE TOP OF THE OCEAN'S FOOD CHAIN. THEIR ONLY NATURAL PREDATORS ARE PEOPLE.

predators in check, which helps to sustain the right balance of predators and prey at each level in the chain. Sharks may also pick off diseased animals in a group which keeps a population healthy. They also provide a clean-up service by eating the remains of dead creatures.

Studying sharks

Scientists are gradually learning more about the importance of sharks. Some of what we know comes from studying them in aquariums. Increasingly, however, sharks are studied in the wild where divers can observe their behaviour in a natural habitat.

COD EAT SMALLER FISH, SUCH AS HERRINGS.

Some individual sharks, such as great whites and basking sharks, can be recognized by their scars and markings. Their behaviour can then be observed and filmed from a boat, using a waterproof camera on a pole to see underwater.

MANY FISH EAT PLANKTON – THE LAST LINKS IN THE CHAIN. PLANT-LIKE PLANKTON USE THE SUN'S ENERGY TO MAKE FOOD.

Tagging

One way to gather information on shark migration is to tag them. Researchers attach identification tags to sharks' fins. Then, if the sharks are spotted or caught by fishers, they report back to the research team saying when and where they found them.

Another method involves fitting sharks with electronic transmitters. These can be attached to a shark's skin or fins, or even placed inside its gut. The route the shark takes can then be tracked using receivers. As the shark swims into range, the receiver picks up signals from the transmitter.

Shark movements can also be

A YOUNG TIGER SHARK IS RELEASED AFTER BEING TAGGED.

A TIGER SHARK IS CAUGHT IN A BEACH NET OFF THE COAST OF DURBAN, SOUTH AFRICA.

picked up from space. Tags with satellite transmitters are attached to the shark, so when it surfaces, signals are picked up by a satellite. The information is then retrieved by scientists. More data can be gathered this way, because it's collected even if the shark is never seen.

Tracking sharks helps scientists find out where they spend their time, which, in turn, helps to conserve them.

Sharks are more threatened by us than we are by them, and need help for many reasons.

Sharks at risk

Hundreds of sharks get caught in beach nets put up to protect swimmers from sharks in South Africa and Australia. Sharks are also caught by anglers, people who hunt large fish for sport.

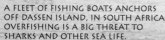

A FLEET OF FISHING BOATS ANCHORS OFF DASSEN ISLAND, IN SOUTH AFRICA. OVERFISHING IS A BIG THREAT TO SHARKS AND OTHER SEA LIFE.

78

However, the biggest threat to sharks and most sea life is commercial fishing. Millions of sharks and their cartilaginous relatives are caught each year for food. You may be surprised to learn that the "rock salmon" used in British fish and chips is actually dogfish, a shark.

Overfishing

But it is the breeding patterns of sharks and rays that make them particularly vulnerable. Because they may take up to six years to reach breeding age – and even then only produce a few pups – fishing can remove them from the sea before they've had a chance to reproduce. This reduces their numbers and can cause a population to be wiped out.

Populations of all types of sea life – including lobsters, sea cucumbers and anything else we like to eat – can plummet if undersized animals are caught before they breed. Careful monitoring, "no fishing" zones, and restrictions on catches can help to maintain fish stocks.

By-catch

Sharks and rays can also be caught by accident when fishers are trying to net other types of fish. This unwanted catch, called by-catch, is wastefully dumped overboard. Some trawlers throw back 40 per cent of their catch – dead. When sawfish, which are endangered, get caught in nets, they are often killed because they're hard to untangle.

100 MILLION SHARKS AND THEIR RELATIVES ARE CAUGHT EVERY YEAR

SCUBA DIVING IS A GREAT WAY TO SEE UNDERWATER LIFE, BUT CARELESS DIVERS CAN DAMAGE CORAL IF THEY KICK THE REEF WITH THEIR FINS.

WASTE WATER POURS OUT OF A PIPE ONTO A BEACH IN THE UK.

Wrecking reefs

Fishing can also damage coral reefs which are home to many sharks and other sea creatures. In southeast Asia people sometimes use home-made dynamite to blow up reefs. The dead fish float to the surface where they are easily collected. Fish are also caught by squirting cyanide into nooks and crannies. Woozy fish are revived and sent off to unscrupulous dealers either for the home aquarium trade or for live tanks in restaurants. Such activities are illegal. Now local communities are encouraged to look after reefs so there will be fish for the future.

Whole reefs can be ruined if soil washes into the sea from building sites or badly farmed land. Soil clouds the water, starving corals of the sunlight that is crucial to their growth.

Nasty chemicals

Pollutants, such as industrial chemicals and metals like mercury, also find their way into the sea via rivers. Other pollutants are discharged directly into the sea or onto beaches by pipelines. This damages sea life, especially once pollutants get into the food chain. For example, if a large fish eats many small contaminated fish, the chemicals are passed along the food chain, and build up in the large fish. Pollutants can affect the development and growth of a creature or make it prone to disease. It can even change it from male to female, or visa versa.

WEIRD WORLD
SHARK FINS ARE HIGHLY VALUED IN SOME ASIAN COUNTRIES FOR SHARK FIN SOUP. SHARKS ARE KILLED JUST FOR THEIR FINS, OR ARE LEFT TO DIE ONCE THE FINS HAVE BEEN CUT OFF.

Oil spills

We can't see most sea pollution but oil spills are impossible to hide. These happen when the supertankers used to transport oil run aground, causing oil to leak into the surrounding seas. The oil floats on the top of the water and can poison animals that swallow it. Seashore creatures are smothered by oil and can't breathe. Spilled oil damages bird feathers and seal fur, making them lose their waterproofing, and causing death.

An oil spill can create a breakdown of the food chain. For example, if oil reaches a rocky shore, its toxic effects weaken the limpets and sea snails living there. They then

loose their footing and slip off the rocks. Without these grazers the green seaweed takes over, smothering the rocks.

L oad of rubbish

Another problem affecting sea life is the disposal of rubbish. Think how much stuff you throw away every day. Well, that rubbish has to be disposed of somewhere. Burning it can send pollutants into the air that eventually end up in the sea. Burying it in landfills (big holes in the ground) can take away

LOG ON...
Learn more about marine
conservation at: www.mcsuk.org

wildlife habitats. Plastic rubbish often ends up in the sea by being blown off the land, carried by rivers, or illegally dumped from boats. Plastic takes a long time to breakdown and can entangle sea life.

G et involved

But it is not all doom and gloom. People are gradually learning more about sharks and their role in the sea, and attitudes are changing. Good news for sharks is that they are now appreciated alive instead of dead. There are efforts to release sharks from beach nets while they are still breathing. More anglers are joining the campaign to safeguard sharks and are letting them go once they've caught them.

If you want to see sharks and other sea creatures, visiting an aquarium is a good idea. These are good places to start to learn about sea life, and how to get involved in conservation work. Find out about places you can visit, and conservation groups you can join, at the end of this book. Everyone can do things

VOLUNTEERS HELP CLEAN UP A SPILL FROM AN OIL TANKER, JESSICA, NEAR THE GALAPAGOS ISLANDS IN 2001.

to help look after the sea and its amazing creatures.

What you can do

• Find out about the sea and its creatures to understand why it needs protection.

• Go on a nature ramble with someone who'll tell you about sea life. Look at critters lurking in rockpools and at shells on the beach. If you like watching marine creatures, remember that crabs and fish left in a bucket die. Look at creatures but always put them back in the sea.

• Take your rubbish home from the beach. Buried litter soon comes back to the surface. Be aware that plastic can kill. The plastic rings that hold cans of drink together are particularly dangerous. Cut through the rings so they can't strangle sea creatures.

• Don't touch or step on corals. It damages them, and can cut or sting you.

• Never buy souvenirs made of coral, shells, or sharks' teeth.

• Recycle. This can also save energy – especially recycling aluminium cans because mining and processing aluminium uses lots of energy. Recycling also cuts down the amount of rubbish that needs to be disposed.

• Save energy. Wear a sweater instead of turning the heating up. Walk or cycle instead of taking the car. This way, we can cut down the amount of fossil fuels transported or burned.

KIDS TAKE PART IN A BEACH CLEAN-UP IN THE UK.

REFERENCE
SECTION

Whether you've finished reading *Sharks*, or are turning to this section first, you'll find the information on the next eight pages really useful. Here are all the facts and figures, background details, and unfamiliar words that you'll need. You'll also find a list of websites and organizations you can contact – so, whether you want to surf the net or search out more facts, these pages should turn you from an enthusiast into an expert.

FISH CLASSIFICATION

In order to describe how the different species of living things relate to each other, scientists classify them into a series of categories according to the features that they share. The largest category is the kingdom. Sharks and other fish are part of the animal kingdom, which also includes every other animal species. The kingdom is divided into smaller categories, which are further divided until individual species are reached. The smaller the category, the more features the animals in it have in common. This chart shows the classification of the shortfin mako shark.

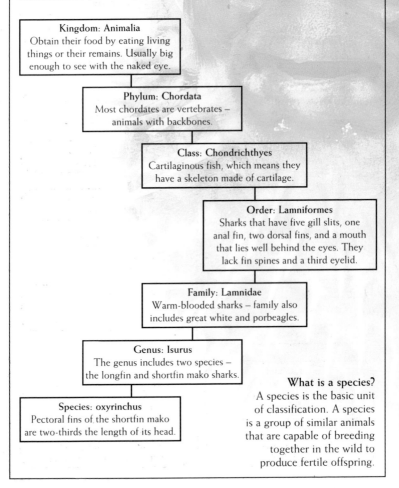

Kingdom: Animalia
Obtain their food by eating living things or their remains. Usually big enough to see with the naked eye.

Phylum: Chordata
Most chordates are vertebrates – animals with backbones.

Class: Chondrichthyes
Cartilaginous fish, which means they have a skeleton made of cartilage.

Order: Lamniformes
Sharks that have five gill slits, one anal fin, two dorsal fins, and a mouth that lies well behind the eyes. They lack fin spines and a third eyelid.

Family: Lamnidae
Warm-blooded sharks – family also includes great white and porbeagles.

Genus: Isurus
The genus includes two species – the longfin and shortfin mako sharks.

Species: oxyrinchus
Pectoral fins of the shortfin mako are two-thirds the length of its head.

What is a species?
A species is the basic unit of classification. A species is a group of similar animals that are capable of breeding together in the wild to produce fertile offspring.

KEY SHARK AND RAY ORDERS

Scientists classify sharks, rays, and other fish into groups according to the features they share.

Fish

**Class Chondrichthyes –
cartilaginous fish**
Have skeletons made
of cartilage.

**Class Osteichthyes –
bony fish**

**Superclass Agnatha –
jawless fish**

**Subclass Elasmobranchii –
sharks and rays**
Don't have the upper jaw fixed firmly
to the braincase, and have gill slits.

**Subclass Holocephali –
chimaeras**

Shark Orders

Ray Orders

Hexanchiformes –
six- and seven-gill sharks, frilled shark

Rhinobatiformes –
guitarfish

Squaliformes –
dogfish sharks, Greenland shark,
cookiecutters, lantern sharks

Rajiformes –
skates

Pristiophoriformes –
saw sharks

Pristiformes –
sawfish

Heterodontiformes –
horn sharks

Torpediniformes –
electric rays

Orectolobiformes –
wobbegongs, nurse sharks,
bamboo sharks, whale shark

Myliobatiformes –
eagle rays, cownose rays,
stingrays, manta rays

Lamniformes –
great white, porbeagles, makos,
basking shark, sand tiger, threshers,
goblin shark, megamouth

Carcharhiniformes –
reef sharks, tiger shark,
bull shark, blue shark, lemon shark,
hammerheads, weasel sharks,
hound sharks, and cat sharks
(includes lesser spotted dogfish)

Squatiniformes –
angel sharks

SHARK RECORDS

Biggest shark
• The whale shark is the biggest shark and also the biggest fish in the sea. It grows at least 12 m (40 ft) long, and weighs more than 13 tonnes.

Smallest shark
• The dwarf lantern shark, the smallest, grows to 20 cm (7.8 in) long. Other small sharks include the pygmy ribbontail catshark (24 cm [9.4 in] long) and the spined pygmy shark (25 cm [9.8 in] long).

Biggest predator
• The great white shark is the biggest shark that hunts for prey. It grows more than 6 m (9.8 ft) long, and weighs two tonnes.

Most dangerous to people
• The great white shark, with more than 250 unprovoked attacks on humans since 1876.

Biggest tooth ever
• The extinct megalodon shark had teeth about 15 cm (6 in) high from the base to the sharp tip.

Longest tail
• Thresher sharks have tails almost as long as their bodies.

Widest head
• The winghead shark has a head whose width is nearly half the length of its body.

Longest lived
• The spiny dogfish probably lives more than 70 years.

Deepest living
• The Portuguese shark has been recorded from depths of about 3 km (1.9 miles).

Fastest
• The shortfin mako is probably the fastest, with some reputed to reach bursts of speed more than 86 kmh (53 mph).

Longest migration
• Tagging studies show a blue shark travelled at least 7,000 km (4,300 miles).

Breeding rates
• The sand tiger gives birth to only two pups at a time.
• The whale shark carries up to 300 embryos at one time.

Longest pregnancy
• Basking shark pups take more than two years to develop inside their mother.

Most endangered and least known
• The river sharks are the rarest and least known sharks. They are threatened because they live in a small habitat (compared to the sea) which is under pressure from development.

RAY RECORDS

Biggest ray
• The manta ray is the biggest with a wing span up to about 8 m (26.2 ft), and it can weigh several tonnes.

Smallest ray
• The short-nose electric ray grows to about 10 cm (4 in) across.

Deepest living
• The pale ray (a type of skate) lives nearly 3 km (1.9 miles) down.

Most electric
• Torpedo electric ray can generate up to 220 volts of electricity.

Most endangered
• The seven species of sawfish are all endangered because their snouts get tangled up in fishing nets.

Breeding rates
• The spotted eagle ray has one to four pups at a time.
• The torpedo ray gives birth to up to 60 pups at one time.

OTHER SEA CREATURE RECORDS

Most venomous
• The sea snake can kill an adult with a minute dose of venom.

Biggest animal without a backbone
• The giant squid is the biggest at 18 m (60 ft) long from its head to its tentacle tips, and weighs up to 900 kg (1,980 lb).

Biggest animal with a backbone
• The blue whale is the biggest animal that has ever lived on Earth. It can grow more than 30 m (98 ft) long.

Largest crab
• Japanese spider crab has a leg span of almost 4 m (13 ft).

Largest lobster
• The American lobster can grow more than 1 m (3.3 ft) long, from its claws to the tip of its tail, and weighs up to 20 kg (44 lbs).

Deepest living fish
• Abyssobrotula, a deep-sea fish, has been taken from depths of more than 8 km (5 miles).

Largest jellyfish
• An Arctic Lion's Mane jellyfish found washed up on the shore had a bell 2 m (7 ft) wide, and tentacles 36 m (120 ft) long.

Fastest fish
• Sailfish have reached speeds of 110 kmh (68 mph).

OCEAN ORGANIZATIONS

The Shark Trust

The Shark Trust promotes the study, management, and conservation of sharks, skates, and rays. *Shark Focus* magazine has photographs, information, and the latest shark conservation news. You can even adopt a shark!
c/o National Marine Aquarium
Rope Walk
Coxside
Plymouth PL4 0LF
www.sharktrust.org
E-mail: enquiries@sharktrust.org

Marine Conservation Society

UK-based charity that involves people in projects including beach clean-ups. Visit their website for great information on marine wildlife and the environment.
9 Gloucester Road
Ross-on-Wye
Herefordshire HR9 5BU
www.mcsuk.org
E-mail: info@mcsuk.org

WWF-UK

WWF is the world's largest conservation organization. Visit their website to check out what the UK branch is doing for marine conservation.
Panda House
Weyside Park
Godalming
Surrey GU7 1XR
www.wwf-uk.org
E-mail:
wwf-uk-supportercare@wwf.org.uk

The Coral Reef Alliance

Promotes coral-reef conservation worldwide by supporting protection efforts and raising public awareness.
2014 Shattuck Avenue
Berkeley
California 94704
USA
www.coral.org

OTHER USEFUL WEB LINKS:

Environment Australia

Good information on sharks, Australian marine conservation, and links to other websites.
www.ea.gov.au/coasts/species/sharks

FishBase

A database with detailed information on sharks and other fish.
www.fishbase.org

IUCN's Red List (International Union for Conservation of Nature)

To find out more about endangered and threatened sharks and rays go to their website and search under the name of the shark or ray.
www.redlist.org

Natal Shark Board

The Natal Shark Board services shark nets along beaches in South Africa. It has an education programme on safe swimming, and the biology of sharks.
http://shark.co.za

Extreme Science
Find out all sorts of fun facts and figures in the "creature world" section on this website.
www.extremescience.com

The Pelagic Shark Research Foundation
Useful information on sharks.
www.pelagic.org

WildAid
This US-based, non-profit organization is currently campaigning against shark finning and overfishing.
www.wildaid.org/programs/shark.htm

University of Hawaii
Information on coral reefs of Hawaii and excellent links to other coral reef websites.
www.coralreefnetwork.com

San Diego Natural History Museum
Plenty of photographs, and facts and figures about sharks.
www.sdnhm.org/kids/sharks/

NOVA online
Stacks of shark information. Also stories of people's close encounters with sharks.
www.pbs.org/wgbh/nova/sharks/world/

VISIT AN AQUARIUM

If you would like to see sharks, rays, and other sea creatures, or you'd like to learn more about marine conservation, you might like to visit an aquarium:

London Aquarium, UK
www.londonaquarium.co.uk

National Marine Aquarium, Plymouth, UK
www.national-aquarium.co.uk

The Deep, Hull, UK
www.thedeep.co.uk

Monterey Bay Aquarium, California, USA
www.mbari.org

New England Aquarium, Boston, USA
www.neaq.org

Seattle Aquarium, USA
www.seattleaquarium.org

Sydney Aquarium, Australia
www.sydneyaquarium.com.au

Nausicaa, Boulevard Sainte Beuve, 62200 Boulogne-sur-Mer, France

Oceanopolis, Port de Plaisance du Moulin blanc, 29 275 Brest Cedex, France

Oceanario de Lisboa, Lisbon, Portugal
www.oceanario.pt

GLOSSARY

Barbels
Feelers on the tip of a shark's or other fish's snout. Used to feel or taste food.

Bony fish
A group of fish with bony skeletons, overlapping scales, and a flap covering their gills.

Buoyancy
The ability to stay afloat.

Cartilage
A gristle-like tissue that makes up the skeleton of sharks and rays. Can be strengthened by minerals.

Claspers
A pair of structures on the belly of a male shark or ray which are used to transfer sperm into the female's body opening (cloaca).

Cloaca
A body opening used for both reproduction and passing out wastes.

Chimaeras
A group of strange-looking fish related to sharks and rays. Named after the monster in Greek mythology who was part goat, part lion, and part serpent.

Courtship
Actions of a pair of animals that encourage them to mate.

Crustacean
Animals without backbones, like crabs, which possess jointed legs and a tough outer covering.

Cyanide
A poison used to temporarily paralyze fish.

Denticles
Tooth-like scales on a shark's skin. These give skin a rough texture.

Excreting
Passing out wastes.

Electrosense
The ability of sharks and rays to detect weak electric signals produced by other organisms.

Electronic transmitter
A device that sends out radio signals.

Embryo
A developing baby animal before birth or hatching.

Estuary
Where a river enters the sea and the water is a mixture of seawater and freshwater.

Feeding frenzy
A group of sharks snapping wildly at food, and even each other.

Fertilization
When a sperm meets an egg and a new life begins.

Fin spines
Spines in front of the back (dorsal) fins in certain types of shark, such as spiny dogfish and horn sharks. They can also occur on several fins in some bony fish, such as scorpionfish.

Food chain
A series of organisms that eat one another beginning with plants and finishing with top predators.

Gills
Thin-walled structures containing blood vessels. Allow sharks and other fish to breathe by absorbing oxygen from the surrounding water, and passing out carbon dioxide.

Gill slits
Openings on the side of a shark's head, or underside of a ray, through which seawater exits after oxygen is extracted by the gills.

Gill rakers
Bristle-like structures on the sides of the gills of sharks and other fish that

sieve water passing to the gills. Used in basking sharks to filter plankton.

Habitat
A place where an organism lives.

Iris
The coloured part of the eye. It surrounds the hole called the pupil.

Lateral line
A line along the side of a shark or other fish that has cells with tiny hairs. These pick up vibrations made by animals or objects in the water.

Light spectrum
The visible wavelengths of light from violet to red.

Light receptors
A group of cells that can detect light.

Mermaid's purses
The horny egg cases of certain types of shark and ray.

Migrate
To make a seasonal round trip from one area to another – often for feeding and breeding.

Nutrients
Substances that help an organism to grow.

Overfishing
Catching too many fish so that there are not enough left to breed and replenish stocks.

Parasites
Organisms that feed on, or in, other organisms causing them harm.

Pectoral fin
The first set of side fins on a shark or other type of fish's body.

Pincers
Claws on crab, lobster, or other crustacean mainly used to cut, crush, or pick up food.

Plankton
Small organisms that drift in water.

Pollutants
Harmful substances that contaminate the air, water, soil, or food.

Pupil (eye)
The hole or slit in the centre of the coloured portion of the eye (iris) that lets in light.

Roe
The ovary of a sea creature, such as a fish or a sea urchin, which contains eggs.

Scavengers
Animals that feed on dead animals or waste.

Shark pups
The young of sharks after birth or hatching.

Species
The basic unit of classification that defines a group of organisms that share many features and which can breed with one another.

Submersible
A vehicle that can carry people down to the depths of the sea.

Spiracle
An opening behind the eyes of a shark or a ray through which it can take in water to breathe.

Swim bladder
A gas-filled structure in bony fish that helps them control their buoyancy.

Tagging
Attaching a numbered tag to a shark or other animal. Some tags have the ability to transmit signals.

Tentacles
Long flexible structures around the mouth of jellyfish, anemones, squid and octopuses.

Umbilical cord
A tube-like structure connecting an unborn human or shark baby to its mother's blood supply.

Venom
A poison produced by an animal and injected or jabbed into a person or animal by a sting or a bite.

INDEX

CREDITS

Dorling Kindersley would like to thank:

Marcus James for initial design concept, Robin Hunter for design help, and Chris Bernstein for the index.

DK illustrations by:

Ann Winterbotham and Dominic Zwemmer.

DK photography by:

Geoff Brightling, Jane Burton, Andy Crawford, Michael Dent, Philip Dowell, Andreas Einsiedel, Neil Fletcher, Steve Gorton, Frank Greenaway, Colin Keates, Dave King, David Murray, Brian Pitkin, Steve Shott, and Harry Taylor.

Picture Credits

The publisher would like to thank the following for their kind permission to reproduce their photographs:
a=above; c=centre; b=bottom; l=left; r=right; t=top

Ardea London Ltd: Adrian Warren 38tl.

BBC Natural History Unit:
Jurgen Freund 55bc. David Hall 50–51; Alan James 33tc; Avi Klapfer/Jeff Rotman Photography 28–29b, 85; Jeff Rotman 3, 10–11, 31bc, 78tc.

Corbis: Ralph A Clevenger 12–13; Corbis 70–71; James Marshall 56bl; Lynda Richardson 68–69; Jeffrey L Rotman 30tl, 36–37; Peter Johnson 78–79; Phil Schermeister 60–61; Stuart Westmorland 35bc.

Innerspace Visions/Seapics.com:
Michel Jozon 40bc; Gwen Lowe 36tl; Doug Perrine 43ca, 44tl.

Carl Meyer: 44bc, 77bc.

N.H.P.A.: A.N.T. 53br; G I Bernard 25b; Trevor McDonald 54tl; Tom & Therisa Stack 46–47; Norbert Wu 18b; 72.

Oxford Scientific Films:
Animals Animals/Bruce Watkins 22b; Howard Hall 16–17b; Richard Herrmann 9; Peter Parks 33tr; 77tc; Tammy Peluso 20; Bruce Watkins 59; Mark Webster 14–15b; Norbert Wu 52c.

P A Photos: EPA/PA Photos 82–83.

Geoff Ward: 84bc.

Woodfall Wild Images:
David Woodfall 81tr.

Book Jacket Credits

Front cover: British Museum tr
Back cover: FLPA – Images of Nature: Minden Pictures/Fred Bavendam

All other images © Dorling Kindersley. For further information see:
www.dkimages.com